How To
Start Your
Own Small
Business

Bernard Featherman
and
Andrew C. Featherman

HOW TO START YOUR OWN SMALL BUSINESS

The authors have recounted events, places and names as well as their memories can recall. However, to protect some individuals' privacy, and to prevent conflicts regarding disclosure of certain facts provided herein, some details like names, dates, places or other identifying items may have been changed, or stories may have been modified, to disguise the persons and entities involved. Some artistic license has been taken.

This book and the information in it are provided for general informational purposes only. No express or implied representations, guarantees or warranties are made by the authors or publisher as to the suitability of any information contain herein to any specific situation; nor should such be construed with regard to any completeness, accuracy, availability, reliability or suitability of these contents with respect to data, processes, products, services, templates or website links provided in this book for any purpose. The contents herein are provided "as-is" to the reader. The authors have attempted to fact-check the information, names, dates and websites cited herein, and information that is contained in this book is considered current as of the time of publication, but not beyond. The authors and publisher assume no responsibility for errors or changes that occur after publication. (Sorry if we miss a typo.) The authors and publisher have no control over or any responsibility for any third-party websites, content, or information.

Published and Printed in the United States of America.

This book is dedicated to Dr. Sandra Featherman. A true beauty both inside and out, she was a leader, role model, thinker, sympathetic protector, and the light that shone a shining path in the dark. Her inspiration as a wife and mother is only overshadowed by the difference she made in the lives of tens of thousands of women across the globe that have better educational and career options because of her hard work, her sense of selflessness, and her unyielding, tireless devotion to "others."

I know she understands that she'll have to wait a while before she's handed her autographed copy...

TABLE OF CONTENTS

INTRODUCTION

Welcome to my father's book. The Honorable Bernard Featherman (after all, he was elected Mayor of Highland Beach Florida twice before term limits ended his run) is a man of great ideas. He has started, purchased, owned or run over two-dozen businesses during his lifetime. That's not including the literally 100-plus organizations he joined or ran, like business promotion organizations, Enterprise Zones, local charities like Rotary and Shriners, and religious and charitable organizations. He has been on (or led) condo boards, associations, political parties (he heads his local one now) and worked for the U.S. Government at one time (he was a Small Business Administration Business Ombudsman for the six New England States; unpaid, but prestigious). He was president of a chamber of commerce. He was named Inc. Magazine Entrepreneur of the Year. He led trade organizations (twice President of the Association of Steel Distributors). He had a cable television show in Biddeford Maine for nearly 20 years, and wrote regular weekly/bi-weekly op-ed pieces for several newspapers in Minnesota, Maine, and Florida. He has numerous commendations from, well, basically everywhere, and knew or befriended U.S. Presidents from Ford through "W" (especially "41" in Kennebunkport). And don't get me started as to the hundreds of **personalized** signed photos he has from senators, congress-people, governors, mayors; he knew so many of them personally. And they all knew him. In fact, I joked to someone last month that I couldn't think of anyone he or my mother didn't know or that didn't know them. Neither can anyone else.

He did all this and more because he believes in four things: Charity, Service, Work, and Others. Charity: Those that have the means have the obligation. Service: Always be ready to serve the greater good. Work: Do the hard work necessary and any task is achievable. Others: You must do for others who cannot do for themselves, and help others to do for themselves. These words he learned at Bordentown Military Academy, where he went to school before college. Three things adorned the walls, including "Good Better Best, Never Never Rest, Until You Good Is Better And Your Better Is Best." Also taught to him were "Others" and concepts such as "Be Your Best" and "Always Be Truthful." These were seared into his psyche and became mantras for him in his adult years. He instilled in me these same qualities: Honesty, Service, Work, and Charity

1

towards others less fortunate than myself, and to do and be your best every day. I never forgot these tenets. It is why I donate money and my time to worthy causes such as animal shelters, the Shriners, scholarships for underprivileged female minority students to go to college, and mentoring. It is why I have worked hard for my rewards. All came from his teachings. What a guy!

So why this book? Well, he wants to espouse his ideas to the masses. He also wants something else to add to his inestimable legacy. Thus we invented **Mr. PHIL** (it stands for **M**arketable Idea, **R**ealistic Financials, Business **P**lans, **H**ard Work, and ***Luck***) and this book on how to start a business. It may not be perfect, but provides his ideas on how to do it based on his more than half-a-century of experience doing just that.

My job here is to edit and make sure that his stories don't go too far off on a tangent, and to add data and depth to his concepts and precepts. Ultimately, though, this is a collaboration, but with his name first: the majority are his stories, ideas and experiences, which I found invaluable myself. I too have run over a dozen businesses - and not all made money - but I learned from each one, and overall made more than I lost. Diversification is good, but doesn't always work in business. I also don't want to overshadow him and his 60+ years of experience.

Venture capitalists tend to invest in not one thing but in a dozen; they figure the law of averages means they will win as much as they lose but they invest in start-ups that don't make twice as much but 10 or 100 times as much for them. A $100,000 investment in each of 10 companies costs $1,000,000. But if half fail and the other half increase to $1,000,000 each, then he makes $4,000,000 profit. That's how portfolio theory works. And how venture capitalists get rich.

Well, you can't do that yourself if you're not already rich. You will need to focus on one - and only one – business. I partnered with someone a few years back who wanted to reinvent the wheel, so to speak. His problem was that he not only wanted to sell wheels, but he wanted to run the stores where they were sold, the malls that the stores were in, and control all aspects of each. That's impossible. Ultimately it failed because he couldn't do 25 things at once. For you to be successful in a start-up, you need to focus on just ONE thing: your new business. It will literally take 100% of your time. Or more...

My mother, God rest her soul (she died in 2018) always said that her job as a university president entailed the following; 50% of her time was spent on fundraising, 50% of her time was spent administrating, and the other 50% of her time was spent "putting out fires." Yes indeed, this adds up to 150%. That's how much effort and time you need to put into your new business. When I ran my first real incorporated start-up, I put all my efforts into it. In 3 years I made enough to pay off my home mortgage (22 years early). When, a few years later, I set up my retail copy center business, I worked weekends and nights when I had large jobs to complete (and I had 24 copiers to work with). The theme of "hard work" is going to appear a lot in this book, and with a good reason: without it, you are guaranteed to fail 100% of the time. No great idea, no unlimited financing, no hot product will be successful without the hard work and viable business plan that must accompany your new venture. Luck isn't enough. As the founder and owner, you may end up the only unpaid employee for a while, and you will work harder than everyone else. You will be the first one in the door in the morning and the last one out at night. You will be responsible for counting your revenue and paying your bills. No one will step in to rescue you if you fail or slack off. Yes, owning your own business means you can come in when you want, choose to close any time you like, and answer to no one but yourself. But if you don't put in the effort, you won't have a business to go to each morning.

Protecting yourself before you start ("cover your rear; register here") is important. Funding is even more important. But nothing tops the need for a kick-ass business plan. And working your tail off.

You are about to embark on one of the four most expensive undertakings you will ever make (alphabetically; Business, Car, College, House). For most people, investing in and starting a business is the single most important, risky – and expensive - thing they will ever do. It will literally make or break you. Yes, businesses can start on a shoestring. (Literally, if you sell shoestrings.) But most viable businesses require tens or hundreds of thousands of dollars in initial capital to start them, (or billions if you're Tesla Motors) and even more money later to make them succeed. And this is for a small business. A larger venture could involve millions in seed-capital, and where will it come from?

Then you get a great idea and need to fund and protect it. You, the 20-something Gen-Y: you've just graduated from college or business school and are working in a job you consider a chore rather than a calling. You have all these great ideas that no one cares about that you believe could make millions (billions?) and you think "if they don't want it, maybe I should have a go at it." You probably have lots of student debt, maybe a mortgage, new retirement account, some savings, and a 5-year-old car with 50,000 miles on it that you just paid off last month. Perhaps you just got a modest inheritance from grandma. You've decided to use this as a base to start your dream business, where you will be appreciated and rewarded for your ideas. Then you start it, do something stupid or have bad luck, and you get sued or go bankrupt and whoops, it's all gone. But it doesn't have to be that way.

This book will show you four primary concepts: a Marketable Idea, Realistic Financials, a strong Business Plan, and Hard Work. Luck, the fifth, is not something you can teach or learn: it is random. It is also necessary, but without the first four, it is useless. You will learn how to determine if you have a good idea or a stupid one. You will be shown how to determine if you have capital and where to look for it if you don't. (This book will not guarantee success in raising funds; it will just show you how.) You will be shown the components of a business plan but you must actually write one tailored to your own business idea. And you will be shown how to market, promote, grow, protect, and support your business and ideas, and the amount of work you'll have to do to keep it that way. You'll also hear a few of my father's wonderful stories about how he got his business savvy and what his experiences were before his successes. True, while no book can promise you that you will be successful, it can be a teaching tool that gives you the so-called "working tools" to succeed. It will give you the foundation you need.

What you do with this information, is up to you. If you **Mr. PHIL** it, at least you'll have a viable chance. Then that luck will be useful...

My father was lucky more than he wasn't. So was I. This is because we also worked harder than our employees, customers, suppliers, and investors (where we had any). Do the same and you can be successful too. All it takes is a lot of work and a great idea... and lady luck smiling on you. And never quit on yourself, because YOU CAN DO IT!!!

Oh, One More Thing...

To differentiate and identify when I'm stepping out of my co-author role and voicing a sidebar opinions or explanation which is tangential or confusing, these "sidebars" (after here, of course) will be shown to you in [*Brackets and Italicized*].

Make it happen! Read this book! Start a business!

And GOOD LUCK!!! (Plus work, skill, business plan, more luck…)

- Andrew C. Featherman

(And my Father is STILL not retired…)

FORWARD

Ellen and I greeted her father's sister, Aunt Sandra, and her Uncle Bernard at our front door some 15 years ago. Sandra, a university president and community activist, was very fond of her niece. Bernard was reputed to be a very well connected, highly successful steel industry entrepreneur. The depth of their character has been repeatedly validated throughout ensuing years with acts of magnanimity, insight and optimistic inspiration.

I introduced myself to Bernard as "having paid my dues working in sales for a large bureaucracy" until my former boss became its chief economist (and leading chemical industry economic expert) shortly after the first gas line appeared after the Arab Oil Embargo. Soon thereafter, Dr. Bill Nelson was hired as COO to administer and grow Chase Econometrics, a small (by Bank standards), partially-owned subsidiary of the Chase Manhattan Bank (CMB). Within a month he made "that offer I couldn't refuse" prompting me to madly begin studying the vagaries of finance, statistical analysis and econometric modeling. I was put in charge of the New York operation which included supervising a staff of economists, consultants and account executives that supported newly hired economists in Fortune 500 corporations, financial institutions and government agencies. Revenue eclipsed all previous records. Staff commensurately grew from 4 to 30 as I quickly accepted the offer to expand my territory to include New England, Canada and Mexico. Remember this was after the energy crisis occurred, and supply side economics was the talk of Washington (E.G., Kemp-Roth bill) and the media pundits.

In due course, according to the CMB's Public Relations department, Chase Econometrics became the source of 85% of all media instances worldwide in which CMB was mentioned (including, to the Bank's dismay, when we occasionally took an opposing position on a favored project, client or industry). Senior executives felt compelled to be closer to the source of their publicity. I was the convenient choice but had to be promoted to an EVP in order to have access to internal bank lending meetings and to give economic outlooks and such to prospective clients and Chase's Directors. This culminated when I hosted a client seminar on the world economic outlook that included participation by Henry

Kissinger and Chairman David Rockefeller; Gerald Ford was the Keynote Speaker. After acquiring the remaining equity from its controversial founder, CMB ultimately merged Chase Econometrics into a larger wholly owned subsidiary, Interactive Data Corporation, and the euphoria was over, but only for a short while as I was about to become an entrepreneur.

Eager to see if all that advice we provided at Chase could work on a smaller scale, I chose an opportunity similar to Andrew's Maine copy business. In my case it was a Lancaster, PA copier dealership. Two years later the business grew to 5 locations and revenue rose fivefold to $4.5mn with commensurate gains in profit. Here, I met and partnered with Marlin "Spike" Reedy (a former Howmet Aluminum CFO and passionate owner of a local, 240 acre farm). Spike and I became owners of a variety of small businesses including the copier company, an auto & equipment lessor, a classic auto restoration shop, an interior design studio, among other endeavors.

Late in 1983 there was a reunion dinner party of sorts with the VP of Chase Econometrics' Metals Forecasting Services that resulted in the co-founding of Resource Strategies, Inc. (RSI) via an agreement specifying that RSI:

*"(m)ust utilize **Chase Econometrics'** worldwide macroeconomic data gathering and modeling to support the metals and mining client revenue base with Chase's existing multidisciplinary team of analysts and consultants who integrate economics, industry expertise and technical judgment to produce a wide range of business advisory services for the world's metals and mining industry."*

Existing revenue adequately supported existing staff, infrastructure and some of the principals' reduced salaries. A separate partnership (of principals) purchased our office condo, and we were in business - again - albeit on a smaller scale. No money changed hands. We extended banking relationships with Lancaster banks. Our office equipment, furniture, computers and copiers were leased from our leasing business. Spike was our accountant. (See Chapter 2 on Swapping Services for Money.)

As our reputation grew, so did the diversity of special projects--Contract

8

Evaluations, M&A, Expert Testimony, Financial and Political Risk Analysis, Feasibility Studies, Competitiveness Analysis of Aluminum Smelters, Rolling Mills, Beverage Can Plants and Electric Utilities. Maritime Strategies International (MSI), a London-based consultancy that forecast trade volumes, vessel values and freight rates was also successfully founded.

One notable project was for Bonneville Power Administration (BPA), a self-funding DOE government entity whose dam in 1990 provided electricity for 11 aluminum smelters in the Pacific Northwest. Aluminum is a commodity whose price can halve or double over the course of a business cycle. Electricity was about 1/3 the cost of aluminum with alumina and *costly* US labor accounting the balance. Electric power is most efficiently generated on a continuous basis without interruption. In an effort to stimulate BPA's continuous production, RSI proposed to link the price of electricity to the price of metal, thereby reducing the cost when metal pricing was low, and increasing it when it was high. A similar strategy was applied to the labor contracts. Smelter competitiveness thereby moved down on the industry's supply curve, and BPA's operational efficiency improved. This strategy was successfully repeated with Hydro-Quebec for Alcan in Canada, Electricite de France for Aluminium Pechiney in France, among others. Today only one Alcoa smelter in Washington is still operating in the region, the result, I suspect, of Russian and Chinese owned and subsidized production and the reluctance of labor unions to negotiate variable pay. Pity....

Several times in his book, Bernard refers to the Better Business Bureau (BBB). I have had the pleasure to serve on the BBB Southeast Florida Board of Directors locally for 26 years, 18 of which were as its 6-term Chairman. I also concurrently served 9 years on the parent organization Board, the Council of Better Business Bureaus (CBBB) in Washington DC including terms on the Executive and Audit Committees and as Chairman of a Task Force that acquired Mobile Giving Foundation.

During my 2nd meeting on the local BBB Board, an opportunity arose to take over the BBB covering Dade and Broward Counties. To my surprise, the West Palm Beach Board was unenthused, perhaps since the Miami based BBB was larger and troubled, and the time to act was short. To quiet the "zealous newbie" the Chair (owner of an Ad Agency)

9

beseeched me to head a Task Force to evaluate whether to pursue expansion with the contiguous operation to our South. With only 4 weeks to submit my findings I agreed to undertake the task under the provision that the Task Force would consist only of an odd number of Directors less than 3 (we had no time to lose), and that I had unlimited access to the WPB CEO (a 25 year BBB veteran) at my office from 2-5pm daily to provide the critical financial, marketplace and staffing insights I lacked but needed to develop the algorithms underpinning the proforma forecast model.

The next Board Meeting was devoted to evaluating the business plan, including monthly (1st year) and annual (5 year) P&L and Cash-Flow forecasts with corresponding Balance Sheets for optimistic, pessimistic and a most likely scenario. Following my presentation the Board voted unanimously to proceed with the acquisition; it immediately doubled the client base, revenue stream and territorial reach while increasing net income to profitable levels never before attained. The Puerto Rico and Caribbean territories and two office buildings were added shortly thereafter completely transforming the influence and significance of this BBB. I was also elected to be the next Chairman.

The Bureau's CPA was most complimentary of the scope of work and incorporated it verbatim into the BBB budget. For this BBB (and many others subsequently, I suspect) this was the first time this kind of analysis had been undertaken. It happened utilizing the type of financial planning described later in Chapter 9. There is simply no substitute for maintaining a full understanding of the financial implications of actions taken during the course of running your business, like in Chapter 6.

In conclusion, Bernard wrote a practical book that will instinctively enlighten the potential and the seasoned entrepreneur with insights that instill best practices and business discipline. One example from Chapter 5: I now know that Enterprise Zones exist to provide economic, tax and other incentives to small businesses. It has been an honor to write this Foreword. I can hardly wait to read what Bernard has to say in his next book.

Kenneth Hanby, President, PTI Consulting, Inc.

Past Chair, Southeast Florida Better Business Bureau

CHAPTER ONE
Who Wants To Be An Entrepreneur?

This is a book about how you can start a small business and make more money for yourself. This is not a book on how to become a millionaire overnight, because only 20% of small businesses that are started have lasted over 5 years in business.

This is a book about being in your own business and developing a business plan to follow like a roadmap. Your success could be the result of 90% hard work, 10% luck and 100% of your attention by being involved in the business. You could be one of the 20% of small businesses that lasts over 5 years and succeeds.

But there is a risk in starting a small business. You have to take the time to learn what the book teaches you on how to setup a business plan, where to get money, what legal steps to start your business in operation and how to deal with banking connections. Since 80% of small businesses fail before five years, you should make knowing the information supplied in this book a must.

There are well over 20 million small businesses (generally defined as less than 250 employees or less than $10 million dollars in sales) alive and kicking in America today. While nearly 90% of these businesses employ 10 or fewer people, many are comprised of just one (above 80%) or two - usually the founder(s) - and opportunities for such entrepreneurs are greater than ever before. Online providers and social media sites like Facebook, Twitter, Google and Instagram have opened up marketing for Small Businesses in new ways from even a decade ago; sometimes becoming de-facto salesrooms for new businesses.

I was a young man when I first started my own small business. I learned what to do and not what to do, by trial and error. However, while I and others could do so in an age prior to online marketing and sales, you cannot "wing it" by trial and error in today's business world and be successful. You must understand business plan procedures, have knowledge of the products or services you want to sell, and be able to obtain the necessary financial sources to start a small business. You need savvy in areas as diverse as finance, marketing, management, and internet technology. So how does a person become successful today? The simple answer to success today is that you have to know WHAT to do, and HOW to do it.

Years later, I started lecturing about business formation to graduate and undergraduate college students, as well as speaking at seminars geared towards those already out in the business world. Attendees who were interested in starting their own small businesses were both male and female, spanned all ages from students to retirees, and crossed all social and economic groups. The attendees included part time and full-time workers, and those jobless who had been laid-off or terminated. All of them shared one key goal: to make a better income then they presently were (or just to earn a livelihood at all), by learning the elemental steps needed to start their own small business.

I found the most interesting questions were asked when I spoke at a Native American Community College in Minnesota. Most of the people who came to hear the seminar - whether young or old or working or not - were lower middle-class families with a deep desire to get answers to their questions about how to succeed, so they could make a better life for themselves and their children than they presently had.

So many people who came to hear me speak over the years felt they would be trapped in low paying jobs in the future, with no way to get out of it, unless they had what we'll call the five "golden keys" of entrepreneurial success, or **Mr. PHIL.** It stands for a **M**arketable Idea, **R**ealistic Financials, A Top-Flight Business **P**lan, **H**ard and **I**ntense Work, and **_Luck_**, which we'll delve into later.

Entrepreneurship and small business growth is an exciting venue in the economic expansion of America today. It can be applied to all kinds of enterprises: retailing, wholesaling, manufacturing, service industries, consulting and home-based small businesses. The topics covered are preparing a business plan, marketing ideas, business financing and where to get money for your business, including how to deal with your banker; whether to buy an existing business, start a new business, or buy a franchise. It includes legal requirements and business organization options (i.e. sole proprietor, partnership, corporations, etc.). And it also includes a sobering truth: absent hard work, you'll fail.

No matter what your age, young in your twenties or 50 years or older, if you have business or job skills and out of work, divorced or simply empty nested, why not try something new like starting your own small business. Even with inexperience in the field you enter, you can learn by getting involved in the product or services you want to be in, by working hard and long hours, with 100% of your time devoted to your enterprise.

Well, who am I? Let me tell you about myself. My name is Bernard Featherman. Like my son Andrew [*who helped me write this book and whose comments will be found in italicized brackets like this*], I am an entrepreneur, both in spirit and in practice. You could also call me a wheeler-dealer who has owned more than just a few small businesses. You could call me a workaholic (most of my friends and family do), a planner, a risk taker and a small business millionaire. I'm all of those things and I've even flunked retirement three times (or is that four now), on the way to doing it.

I march to a different drumbeat than most entrepreneurs, but I still mostly fit the general profile of one anyway. I say "mostly" because I am liberal in social values, but conservative in fiscal matters. My belief is in diversity and in equal opportunity for all, but also lowering of taxes on, and less regulation of, business.

Most entrepreneurs are very conservative and republican in nature, but that's where I'm different: my political party affiliation. Most business owners are on the opposite side of the political spectrum from me. I too am a conservative businessman, but a past national officer of the Democratic Party, and yet a successful small businessperson as well.

I have owned many small businesses with my brothers over the years, allowing me to be both financially comfortable and socially popular. Our enterprises included steel distribution centers, manufacturers of industrial storage products, retailers of new and used machinery, a retail office furniture chain, and the buying and selling of various commercial and industrial businesses and commercial real estate facilities. I was even an owner of a cemetery in Pennsylvania, where you could say I handled customers in rather grave situations, literally!

We invested in start-up companies, purchased equity in existing businesses, and acquired business operations that included industrial and commercial assets, distressed inventory, and bankrupted businesses. We bought real estate when we could buy it cheap, and fixed it up and rented it out or sold it at a profit. And in our continuous search for new business ideas and new investments, we were constantly involved in seeking dependable, long term money sources to do it.

Along the way, I've had time to be involved in the political world, as well as the helping others to develop and nurture their own businesses. I was a past Finance Chair of the Pennsylvania Democratic State Committee and a former National Chairman of the Small Business Council of the Democrat National Committee in Washington, D.C.

In 1990, I was awarded as the Entrepreneur of the Year Award: Supporter of Entrepreneurship Category, co-issued by Inc. Magazine and Ernst & Young at their Scottsdale, Arizona annual meeting. The following year, the US Small Business Administration awarded me their Entrepreneur of the Year category award. And when I retired for the third time I got busy again. In 2011 I was elected Mayor of the Town of Highland Beach, Florida. Three years later, the residents re-elected me for another full 3 years (unopposed, by the way), which allowed me to serve the maximum term limit of 6 years.

As an entrepreneur, I have had many credit cards, private dining club memberships, and large number of gas and department store credit cards. One of the cars I currently drive (or are chauffeured in) is a leased Mercedes-Benz that I trade in every three years. I've owned flats race horses and partnered in stud breeding horses. In fact, I have had several personal checking and savings accounts at several leading banks.

Now, not everything we invested in or started made money. Some of them failed. They failed because they were the right idea but at the wrong time, or we or someone connected to it underfunded it, or it was not run properly (where someone else was in charge and not us) or sometimes it simply was a great idea and we did everything right but something out of our control made it underperform - or flat out fail.

I tell you all these things not to boast, but for a reason: each of you can do the same as I did, if you are properly motivated, properly financed and properly skilled in the product knowledge and correct business strategies in the field you go into business. Let me say again, to be successful in a startup small business is 90% hard work and 10% luck. The fact is only 20% of all startup businesses will survive after five years, so a good business plan is important. With a solid business plan, you have a 4- or 5-times better chance of success in your endeavor, and by creating the plan in the first place, you will have a clearer understanding of whether or not you are likely to succeed in what you are attempting.

Everything we personally did or have done in business was commenced with a well thought out and solid business plan. We knew where we wanted to go and how we were going to get there. We started out like each one of you can do, when you start a new business or expand an existing business.

It was no accident that we used credit cards (and bank loans). The first principle in running a successful business is to use other-people's money. Think finance and credit when you think of spending money with a credit card, although you still are responsible to pay it off.

It was no accident we leased cars. Leasing, as opposed to owning, is a 100% deductible business expense item on taxes. Why depreciate and get only part of the benefit, when you can deduct and get it all?

It was no accident that we owned race horses, hotels and apartment houses. (Ok, some of it was…) Investors can take substantial depreciation allowances against income to reduce income tax payments, and it is legal and legitimate as long as you follow the tax code and the rules. (And are willing to lose money on an investment.)

It was no accident that we deposited at several banks and not just one. Why? So that we could borrow money from one bank and pay off loans due to a different bank. It let us establish relationships with each bank so that we could borrow more easily or have a new source of funds if there was a problem with one bank: we could just switch to another. We created lines of credit, both long term and short term for business loans, letters of credit or mortgages. Also, you never know when you need a new banker or a second choice, so prepare one.

If we needed working capital for our businesses, we could remortgage our real estate. Generally, real estate properties appreciate in value over time and later, when you needed more money, most mortgages are partially or mostly paid off due to past payments, while both the market value and the loanable value of the real estate usually rises (in most cases). That is how we did it: we sold or re-mortgaged many properties in order to get new money funds, so we could invest the proceeds for operating cash, purchasing real estate or buying new equipment needed for our business.

It was no accident we were partners in other companies. One example? We needed expertise in automation so we went in partnership with a retired chief engineer of a leading Fortune 500 company. We took orders and collateralized them against a working capital loan to start another small business, a computer-controlled machinery distributorship that served the metal fabricating industry. Partnering allowed us to share investment costs, and gave us a person that "had our back" when we needed it. Remember that your partner is usually disposed to being just as frightened of failing as you are, so they will be just as incentivized to make sure it succeeds and that everyone does their job. Especially if they also have money at risk, which they should. Remember: all partners should have "skin in the game" for incentive.

In the 1970's we invested with several people who wanted to start their own business. One of these involved several salespeople employed by a leading company in their field which was rumored to be relocating operations from their then-present location. These people contributed the same amount to as we did, so each would have the same stake, and the same risk. That investment grew from a fledgling business in the first year to a multi-million-dollar success later on.

Another example is when we bought a 21-unit apartment house by putting 10% down, which we borrowed on a mortgage from a bank, and then received a second "takeback" mortgage from the seller. We fixed up the property, raised the rents, and made our 10% down money back in four months. That is the way to make profit, without involving any of our own investment money.

Many small businesses are simply established with the leverage of finances, knowledge of the subject from all angles and working your business plan to be successful.

It was no accident that we were members of several trade and for profit 501(c)(3) organizations in order to learn about things going on in the field we were interested in, by attending seminars for ideas on concerns to be solved, as well as our friendly contact with non-competitors and competitors alike in the industries in which we did business. We traded, sold or even made confidential buying swaps on products with them (but not insider information).

It is no accident that we do charitable and civic work - for two reasons. One is altruistic, while the other is somewhat self-serving. I promised my parents that I would give at least 10% of my time as a volunteer and in charitable organizations, to help others less fortunate than me. The other reason is the exposure I have gotten that helped put me in contact with area and national leaders that could benefit us with business advice, financial and social support.

I got involved with charitable and for profit 501(c)(3) organizations, including as a board member of organizations like the Rotary Club, American Red Cross, and March of Dimes. I was appointed by three different U.S. Presidents to terms on the White House Conferences on Small Business in Washington, D.C. I was two-time national president of the Association of Steel Distributors (for USA and Canada), State Treasurer of Pennsylvania's Association of Retarded Citizens as well as being the President of its Philadelphia chapter, Chair of the Mental Health and Retardation Board for the City and County of Philadelphia as appointed by three consecutive Mayors, and was a member of Business Advisory Boards for three separate universities. I also was the Chair of one of the four sub-committees of the Palm Beach County, Florida, Criminal Justice Commission.

My two brothers and I were equal – and united - partners in all our business dealings, which included start-ups, buying whole existing businesses, and as investors (silent or otherwise) in other companies. Many deals did exceptionally well, and others did not. Besides industrial and commercial businesses, our investments included a hotel, office furniture store chain, Bed and Breakfast Inn, apartment houses, and commercial and other real estate. Everything we did we did by unanimous decision. If you invest with partners you have to be able to trust them. I and my brothers trusted each other and everything we did we did together as a unit, or not at all. That cost us some money by leaving deals on the table, but it saved us heartache when one did not like a deal that ultimately proved to be a money-loser. Remember that you must have a united front: never cheat your partners, because you ultimately cheat yourself when you do.

Starting as a teenager, my life pyramided into an entrepreneurial mode. It grew from shining shoes for campers in summer camp, to cutting neighbors' lawns in the Spring and Fall Seasons of the year and shoveling snow from houses and sidewalks in the winter.

At the beginning, those were my salad days, when I was green in judgement. Success really flourished as I volunteered with a number of 501(c)(3) charitable and business organizations. It helped me build friendships with other board members and staff members on these organizations. It continued to be an avenue for advice and suggestions on future business ideas.

Years later, when my wife became President of University of New England, we moved to Kennebunkport, Maine from Minnesota where she had been Vice Chancellor at University of Minnesota in Duluth. She remained President of University of New England in Maine for 11 years, after which I retired for the second time. It was so boring to relax and do nothing that I yearned to be active again.

During this time, I was asked (and accepted) to be the President/Executive Director of the Biddeford-Saco Chamber of Commerce in York County, Maine. I also became an OP-ED business columnist for the Journal Tribune newspapers for over 15 years (writing as recently as 2015) and hosted a half hour TV show in Maine called BUSINESS TODAY, on the Channel 3 Cable TV station. And - you probably guessed it - during that time I continued to make more business deals.

HERE ARE SOME OUTSTANDING ENTREPRENEURES THAT STARTED BUSINESSES AT DIFFERENT AGES IN THEIR LIFE. YOU CAN SEE THAT AN ENTREPRENEUR CAN GO IN BUSINESS AT ANY AGE - AND SUCCEED!

Steven Jobs. At 21 years old he started Apple Computers.

Michael Dell. At 19 years old he started Dell Computers.

Ted Waitt. Ted started Gateway Computers with a $10,000 loan from his grandmother.

Henry Ford. Henry was 45 when the Ford Model-T came out.

Ray Kroc. At age 53 Ray bought a McDonald's franchise and built it into one of the world's franchise leaders.

Margaret Rudkin. At 45 years old she was the woman who started Pepperidge Farms.

Colonel Harland Sanders. The Colonel was 61 years old when he started his Kentucky Fried Chicken franchise chain.

As the saying goes "Acorns don't fall far from the tree." Well, that fits my older son Andrew (my co-author) who was always trying to make extra money. Andrew, who has three degrees from Temple University (BA in Economics, M.B.A. in Operational and Strategic Management, and a Juris Doctor) was always trying to establish a new business or money-making idea. Andrew has a true entrepreneur's spirit. He bought and sold U.S. coins, bills and stamps, swapped odd ball merchandise, collected and sold baseball cards, and held jobs like babysitting, assembling storage lockers sold by one of our companies, and other odd jobs for added income wherever he could. This even when he worked in the family business, starting with sweeping floors and rising to being the chief operating officer of the business. [*Actually, I really DID start out with Acorns... I ran the Acorn Booth at the Philadelphia Flower Show as a junior in High School and made a piddling salary, but I also got high school credit for doing it.*]

As a teen he even worked part time as a stock boy in a local comic book store. He got the job by selling the idea of having his wages taken out in comic books. Naturally, after work he sold those comic books he didn't want or had already read to others, so he made his wages one way, or another.

In Maine, he opened his startup small business, Copycat Print and Copy Center, in the garage of his home, as did many business owners in Maine. He ran it for 3 years before selling the business to pay for his training for his current profession: that of a lawyer admitted in 5 US states. [*It was a pretty large business and I came by it honestly; I had a tuxedo cat named Frisky who copied everything I did. It was really named for him and for the beautiful double-entendre the name made.*)

Now not everybody can just start a business willy-nilly. But with proper direction, anyone actually can. The tools include using combination of background knowledge, contacts to sell to the customer trade you are in, and in learning to act with ethical behavior in doing business with your customers. All this plus Mr. PHIL and some extremely hard work, realistic goals and assumptions, and a bit of luck.

HERE ARE 10 "NEEDS" YOU MUST CONSIDER WHEN YOU WANT TO STARTUP A SMALL BUSINESS

1. You need to learn or know money management skills.

2. You need to set goals, in dollars or units, on sales and future growth.

3. You need to have or to learn marketing skills.

4. You need to write down, in order of priority, the things you have to do in the business.

5. You need to estimate the money you can make in your venture.

6. You need to check your competition.

7. You need to put together a solid, useful Business Plan.

8. You need to be properly capitalized, in real money (not Bitcoin).

9. You need to determine the type of business you want to be in.

10. And, finally, you need to be absolutely certain you will put in the hard work required to succeed!

The New York Times published an article on November 23, 2017 that stated according to government statistics, 99% of American businesses have less than 500 employees, and roughly 80% comprise some 23 million small business enterprises of one kind or another that are one-person operations.

The strength of a small business is to be nimble, to move quickly and to find solutions fast. That means having a small business that can evaluate sales problems, update operating procedures, undertake new marketing directions and fix financial concerns. Successful small business people do not get bogged down on too many committee meetings, excessive paperwork or wasted time efforts. Instead, they act on issues promptly and seek to get results that translate to success.

Small business entrepreneurs are the driving engine that propels innovation and opportunity in sales, technical and marketing areas. Change today is necessary to be competitive and profitable.

You have to be more innovative as a small company grows. You have to create a long-term strategy to utilize related issues, analyze information properly, or fine tune the advantages of software use.

Most smart small business people have their own "think tank" person: themselves; they also have a small but approachable network of mentors, affiliates, and peers who they can ask questions or bounce ideas off of. Their success is measured by the nature of their own vision, not only in user and customer friendliness, but in quick, comparative options, for customers to do business with their company.

Everyone knows that you have to make a profit to stay in business. Sometimes critics of businesses forget that, but you can't stay in business if you lose money continually.

And a lot of businesses do lose money. Tons of it. Estimates are that more than 80% of all new small businesses fail in less than 5 years. This means only about 20 percent make it to 5 years. More than half of all new businesses fail in less than 18 months, and a good portion of those do not even survive their first year. Why? Simple. Economics. Those that survive and thrive usually do so because the owners work long hours at low pay or even WITHOUT SALARY until their business is solid enough to do well and pay them. Those that fail do so because they are undercapitalized; either they miscalculated and started with too little capital, or the owners drew out too much in salary. And many businesses simply fail because their founders fail to do the hard work and put in the long tedious hours required to succeed.

It is indeed a struggle for many small businesses to survive. Still, a lot of politicians around the country argue that businesses make excessive profits. That's not true, of course, except for a rare few that comprise less than a fraction of 1% of the total number of businesses in the country. Otherwise, so many owners would not have to close their restaurants, retail stores or other small businesses when there are economically tough times. The first thing some business people want to do is to clamp down on overhead and squeeze out partial income or temporarily take no income out of their business, in order not to fail and go out of business. But many still fail.

Business owners have to face the fact that they are a minority in this country. They can be out-voted anywhere. When they get favorable legislation or prevent unfavorable laws, it is because business people have gotten very active, worked hard and convinced the rest of the voting public that anti-business legislation hurts everyone. If businesses cannot make a profit, they close and their workers lose their jobs. An added cost is that these entrepreneurs (who risk everything they have) lose it all and most never re-enter the business world as an entrepreneur or owner again, at the cost of future jobs and the resulting tax revenue for governments that often regulate them out of business.

Let's think about it. When government needs more money, they tax businesses, who are usually the smallest and safest group of voters to burden. When people want more government services, someone has to pay. Businesses, big and small, make juicy and easy targets.

Anytime there are strikes, owners of businesses are a real minority. The system is slanted toward labor, not because labor is inherently not worthy, but because there are so many more workers than owners.

First, when city workers go on strike, politicians almost always capitulate, because they need support from these employees to get re-elected. So, they give government workers higher pay increases that are often way out of line with what private industries can afford to pay their employees.

Second, some political activists have expressed the concept of healthy profits as almost immoral. Business owners are vilified as evil for taking salaries that are tens or hundreds of times what their average employee makes. In non-public company cases, this is highly justified because these owners took the risk to gamble everything they owned and would own to bankroll or guarantee the backing of a loan for a business venture that employed not just themselves but other workers who gain their livelihood from this risk. When they succeed (and not all do) they should be suitably rewarded for their efforts. After all, isn't that "The American Way" we keep hearing so much about? Additionally, these owners are continually and personally on the hook to banks for everything they own as long as these loans are in existence. These owners are entitled to be compensated for the enormous risk they take to ensure that these "underpaid" workers are able to cash their paychecks each week whether or not the business has enough sales or revenue collection to cover their checks.

In the past, price-controls and government regulations were directed at controlling costs, which resulted in lower profits for all kinds of businesses. Ask yourself why the control on rising costs of labor and materials, especially on items like energy supply, oil, steel and certain materials are subject to some immutable law that says prices must always go up?

No one should assess fair profits for business, except for owners and investors. If their costs or prices increase too much, they can't sell their products or services. In small businesses if the incentive to invest, innovate and to make a profit is diminished or eliminated by someone taking away that profit because they think it isn't fair for them to have less than you have, then why in the world would anyone willingly invest money or time in a small business? They wouldn't!!!

Rewards for talent, for ideas, and for risk-taking, have led men and women to start small businesses, not to stifle their innovations and economics freedom. Small businesses could leave the marketplace or close entirely if they aren't given a fair opportunity to succeed.

Entrepreneurs are younger today than 20 years ago. They are better educated and very motivated to work for themselves. They know the field they are entering. Most are workaholics, and, are both physically and emotionally strong enough to run a startup small business. They are, by and large, also true risks takers.

We've learned that successful entrepreneurs combine innovation, opportunity and resourcefulness to succeed. They find opportunities to develop their ideas for new services, business needs or consumer products that sell to the public. Entrepreneurs may luck out in what they do, but some ideas just don't pan out.

Most successful entrepreneurs set goals with a Business Plan, not only to make the money but to get "high" on the excitement that makes their dreams come true. A good Business Plan prepares the entrepreneur to move upwards, both with driving ambition, and by working hard, long hours. Entrepreneurs must learn to ask questions, visit people in similar businesses or services for product ideas, and glean pricing and marketing information. Many times, it means taking hold of a situation at the right time and making a fast decision to do something about it. Moving quickly and taking a chance is where that "risk: element comes into play yet again.

Success starts with a well thought out business plan, constantly updated to meet any service, product or design change; hiring capable management people as needed to help run the enterprise, and it should include a realistic marketing plan on what to do. Success ends with taking that plan and putting in the hard work to make it succeed, and taking calculated risks and not poor ones.

Also, you have to think positive. All Of The Time. Even if you have to walk away from a "failure" on a non-profitable venture, you must have a positive attitude. It will give you time to review why the deal didn't work in the first place. Sometimes it is a question of inadequate funding; this tells you to find a new bank, investor, or other source of money, or to get (new?) investment partner(s). Sometimes, it is a matter of tweaking or modifying the Plan, whether it is working or not, to give yourself a better chance to succeed. Sometimes it is a sign that this was a bad plan and you need to find something else. So do it.

The down side of making the jump into entrepreneurship is finding adequate financing money, developing a viable Business Plan, and creating a quality product or service. All this takes a lot of work. Be ready to do that work. Successful entrepreneurs do not give up, even in the face of losing everything.

Small business success in a new company is heavily affected by luck and opportunity, too. Neither stands alone as aggressive, quick action is generally a requirement of business creation. A friend once said his father told him not to marry for money, but go to where it was, when looking for a wife. A small business owner that keeps the right company, in the right industry, puts themselves in a position to capture opportunity and to experience luck. And maybe even a spouse, wealthy or not, too!

How true.

Okay Mr. PHIL, let's go on to CHAPTER 2.

CHAPTER TWO
Swapping Services For Money

When I was a little boy, I thought everyone was in business. My great grandfather owned a circus. My grandfather owned movie theatres and a limo service. My father and his brother had owned a steel foundry that supplied steel angles and caster wheels for bed frame manufacturers, which led to their eventually owning and running a bed manufacturing and steel tubing business. Several of my other uncles and cousins owned specialty retail or wholesaling small businesses, too.

I dreamed that one day I would have my own business. I fantasized being in my own business until that dream became a reality. It started early in my life. My driving force was to make money that could build a business from nothing to something and make it happen successfully.

Becoming a successful entrepreneur takes vision, self-motivation, independent persuasiveness and being a risk taker. You have to adapt to change, in a world where nothing is constant, whether young, old, or in-between.

There is one solution for some folks to consider. They could go into their own home-based business, when they feel burned out on their present job, worried about their job, or have just been laid off. It becomes a good time to rethink about working for yourself in a part-time or full-time small business, from your home.

You need to be familiar with the type of business you want to go in. You are more likely to be successful if you choose as your proposed business something based on a hobby you are familiar with, or in areas for which your skills or trades are abundant in past experience. Perhaps you like gardening. If so, the landscaping business might be your ticket, cutting lawns for people in the summer (and plowing snow in the winter) and could appeal to you as well as provide you a means to earn a living. Perhaps becoming an Uber or Lyft or taxi driver, chauffeuring elderly people for meetings, medical appointments, or doing shopping errands for them, might be great for part or even full-time small business income.

Why not sell products by phone or by Internet, do accounting and bookkeeping services, conduct home tag sales, or do house sitting on weekends for part-time income? These are all jobs available right in your own local area, in which you can ply your trade and start a small business. There are literally hundreds of full or part-time business opportunities you can consider, all by expanding on or honing a skill you already have but have not been using, or retooling yourself for a different trade than you have done before, no matter how old you are.

Why not take the opportunity to start working in your own home-based business? My friend Tom did that, after being laid off from working 20 years for a local service company that downsized due to the economy. Tom worked in customer service at his former company, so he knew how to talk to customers. He decided to start a home-based business to buy and sell service products with which he was familiar. He called companies whose products he had handled and several hired him to do telephone sales and make visits to his former accounts, for which he was to be paid a commission on sales.

Tom did what everyone should do when starting a small business. He created a business plan to work from, and he determined how he would market his services. To keep overhead low and to get a quick start, Tom decided to run his business from home.

Why? Tom did not have to pay any additional rent for outside office space or buy new equipment and furniture: things he already had in his home. He had no travel time to and from work, which saved him quite a bit on gas. In fact, all Tom needed was to repurpose a desk, get an office chair, filing cabinet, computer, photo copier and office supplies. All told, it added up to less than a $1000 investment. Now he could start his business.

Running a home-based small business has its drawbacks and its benefits. What are the drawbacks? Let's start with privacy and professionalism. Working at home has many distractions. Family interruptions by children and pets and background noise when Tom was on the phone or meeting with a client were common. People running in and out of nearby rooms just added to the distractions. Tom needed privacy and the family cooperated, but normally it is not easy. However, there is a way to get help with this problem, by using a simple two-part rule: the "Dress" and "Door" solution. "Dress" as you would as if you were going out to a regular office, and close your office "Door" to create a semblance of privacy. Treat your home office workspace as if it were that of an outside employer. This is a lot like the "dress for the job you want, not the job you have" rule, but translated for use with at-home workspaces.

The benefits of working at home are many, and mostly favor cost and convenience. They include extremely low overhead because you generally don't need to rent your home office from yourself. An added benefit is tax-related: the ability to deduct part of your residence tax, mortgage, and utility expenses - but only if you use that area exclusively for business 100% and there are tax drawbacks when you sell the house. You can also deduct or expense anything else which is used exclusively for your work and is used to generate taxable income, such as phone lines, utilities, computers, copiers, printers, paper, file and storage cabinets, vehicles (if used solely or primarily for work) and other related items. While a professional office would have helped Tom grow faster, it was prohibitively expensive. The cost benefits outweighed the short-term losses from a more professional setting.

But there were still costs. Tom's wife started to solicit web page layouts from the same office space and it was crowded for both of them to work out of the same area. Tom also missed wearing a shirt and tie when doing work at home, because he was not following the Dress and Door protocol from above. Tom also missed being around people because he primarily worked alone at home. But the occasional visits to his customers helped Tom feel more connected to his business, and to the people it served.

Tom needed to schedule his work on a weekly basis in order to reach his business goals. He kept to his business plan and added an important step, to stay at the cutting edge to make his business grow.

Networking.

It was networking that Tom found pays the most dividends in a start-up business. Tom began to volunteer on a pro bono, working for non-profit organizations. As a result, he met other business owners and potential future customers through his newfound connections at these organizations. Tom found out that people like to do business with people they know. Gee, doesn't everybody? Tom got ideas, leads and feedback from these sources. Much of this information solved some of his own marketing problems. As a result of one of these networking meetings, Tom was contacted by his former employer to sub-contract phone work for them. Thus, networking helped Tom grow his business beyond what he could have done on his own.

We need more small businesses to pump prime money into our economy's growth, like Tom is doing.

It seems small businesses survive because they are spartan, tough and competitive. They have to be because they know what the alternative is if they weren't: FAILURE. Small business is big business, but small businesses must be their own advocates to champion their own causes.

Small businesspeople are the backbone of American business, but they are not necessarily synonymous with it. They often decide to let big business fight their battles for them, usually due to the costs. But oftentimes that is a mistake, because while their interests are similar, they are not identical.

How could that be? Well, obviously unless small businesses thrive, big companies won't have adequate outlets through which to sell their products. When small business profits disappear, inventories pile up, cash-flow gets poor and services from small companies to big companies slow down. That is why small and big businesses are tied together. Society cannot survive on "Goliath Inc." alone.

Big business and small business are intertwined in many ways, but not in all ways. Many tax loopholes benefit big business, although it might not appear that way. Some loopholes allow certain sectors of the system to pay less than their share of taxes, which means all the other sectors, including small businesses, have to pay more. And many small business people believe that big business companies buy out small competitors or build their own outlets in order to sell them goods at preferential prices to "category kill" the competition. These acquisitions or creations reap the benefits of parent company credit, planning staff, technical and inside financing knowledge, and reciprocal buying agreements. While small businesses are expected to compete equally in the marketplace, many small companies have no such back up capacity. Sound familiar? You bet it is.

Small businessmen and businesswomen are not against big companies. They are all for them. Almost all small business people would like to be big companies themselves someday, because that's the American dream.

But many small businesses are not big enough right now to forget who they are.

The important thing to remember as small business people is you have to wage your own battles. Especially tax and regulatory battles. These legislative battles seek to change laws from within the political system, not just through complaining to themselves. Small business can't count on big companies to satisfactorily represent their views, any more than they count on unions to do so. Not because either of them are doing wrong, but because their job is to fight for their own special interests. What is necessary or wise for small business people might not be any other group's main concern, interest or consideration. As small business people, you are the only ones who can say what you need in order to compete and survive, and only you are the one who must be willing to work for and fight for your interests. If you don't do it, you can't count on others to do it for you.

Small business can be a powerful voice, but to make it work you must be an active, not a passive part in the process. As a person who started a small business, that is why I got involved in fighting for us.

I love being in business. It is a real challenge to be working for yourself. The first business my younger brother and I started was in our elementary school days. We shined shoes for students (including over a dozen foreign students), in exchange for their foreign stamps on envelopes sent to them from families overseas. We soaked off the stamps from the envelopes, put about 30 stamps in a number 10 size envelope and mailed them to interested stamp collectors for $5 each mail order. We got leads from a four-line classified ad, placed by us in local newspapers. We took care of the ad and postage costs, with monies out of our weekly lunch allowances. We got the $5 in advance before we mailed the stamps, so there were no cash collection problems. I remember splitting almost $200 that first year with my brother on a 50/50 basis. And remember, this was when $200 was enough to buy a used car.

That led us to a second business to consider, shining shoes. As a result of doing one business, along came even a better opportunity for us. We started a shoe shining business at the 8 week-overnight summer camp we attended, which was located near Philadelphia. Word of mouth spread that the Featherman boys shined both camper and counselor shoes, especially needed by campers and their counselors when parents visited their children on weekends.

A customer shoe shining base continued for the following three years of camp seasons. We liked the idea of making our own money. We charged 35 cents an individual shoe or 50 cents per pair. Two tone shoes were double the price. Some weeks we netted almost $20. It's amazing how many young people 10 to 15 years of age would give us two or three pairs of shoes to shine at a time, instead of only one pair. We made almost $125 that first season. Not bad money for two kids 8 and 11 years old. Again, we split it 50/50. And we kept it up during the regular school season to high school students. We shined in the Fall, and we shined in the Spring. It was not a lot of money to a full-time laborer earning wages to pay for a family, but for us it was a lot, and we were on a roll toward more surprises yet to come.

Two years later, after leaving summer camp, we came up with another idea. Let's mow lawns for our neighbors in the neighborhood. At first, we cut local neighbors' lawns ourselves for our own spending money. On the weekends, we built up a list of additional lawn owners in our local areas to be served. Then, we went around to homes in a three-mile radius of where we lived, to personally contact prospective lawn owner customers. I used my bike to get around to see and contact those prospective customers.

As our business was growing, we realized we needed more people than just the two of us to do lawn mowing work, especially outside of our local area. So, we came up with the idea to hire two unemployed men to help do lawn mowing for our customers outside our normal area of coverage. They each had to have their own flatbed pickup trucks to transport their lawn mowers to customer locations. We did in fact hire two men to do that job for accounts that were outside of the three-mile area. We were on a roll again.

Early on, I went around during the late evenings to collect the cash charged for the work done that week on our customers' lawns. Each Saturday afternoon, we would settle up with our two hired workers for work they did that week. The lawn mowing business continued to run successfully.

To earn extra money between college semesters, I drove a Jack 'N Jill Ice Cream truck route in the summer. [*Andrew also sold Jack 'N Jill Ice Cream as a teen, at summer stadium concerts.*] My brother and I shoveled snow off our neighbors' sidewalks and driveways during the winter for spending money. I bought and sold used college textbooks to other college students for their school courses. Money motivated me, but it was not the underlying decision to do things. I learned you must be an active participant in what you do, not just a voyeur, to be successful.

After my third year in college, my father asked me to work at my uncle's steel tubing manufacturing plant in Brooklyn, New York. My father wanted me to get experience in working in a fabricating plant. That is why he asked me to go to a plant that my uncle owned in New York, to learn how to run a steel tube mill machine that made electric welded steel tubing. I could not turn my father's connection down for me to get such a job, so I took the summer off to do it. Little did we know - prior to when our father died many years later - that he and his brother each owned 50% of that company.

I left the supervising of the lawn mowing business to my younger brother and our cousin, and went off to learn how to run machines that made industrial steel tubing.

When I started my new job, I was put under the supervision of a steel tube mill operator who recently came to my uncle's company. He had over 20 years of experience doing the same job at a competitor's steel plant. Being young (and a nephew of the owner) the operator probably thought I was there to take over his job in the near future, so he didn't explain important production processes to me that I could learn on the job, under his supervision. Instead, he had me put steel coils into the coil cradles and take away the finished tubing for storage, without being shown how the important control panel worked, to process the steel tubing at all stages of production.

The tube mill operator was wrong on both counts, on not teaching me and on thinking I was going to take away his job. But about five weeks into my new job, an accident happened that was life threatening to the tube mill operator. A red-hot slither of molten metal broke apart from the welded tubing. It happened at the heater scarfing control station, where he and I were stationed. It headed directly toward the operator's face. With no time to think, I threw my asbestos covered hand upward against the burning metal. It diverted the flow of the hot material away from his head. It prevented a life-threatening (or ending?) accident from happening to him.

The steel slither was so hot that it cut through my asbestos glove, leaving a permanent scar on my hand. My son will attest that I still have that scar. [*Yes. I asked about it. He showed it to me. It's still there. OUCH!*]

The operator knew what I did. It saved his life. During the next two weeks, he taught me all that he knew about the job. Because of this incident, when I went back to the college that fall semester, I was more determined not to work for someone else, but one day to be a boss (working with my two brothers).

When I came back home, I reviewed the lawn mowing business with my brother but received disappointing news. The first few weeks we made about $200 a week, after expenses. Afterwards, some lawns were not done on time, or others not done at all, on the days promised to lawn home owners. One worker showed up drunk on the job and he was sent home. He should have been fired, but he wasn't. Later we also found out that some of the payments were improperly collected by the lawn mowing operators themselves and not turned in to him as they should have been.

We'd forgotten an important rule, that owners must supervise workers on a daily basis; this ensures that customers are happy, workers actually work, and money goes where it is supposed to (to us and not stolen by workers). You can't go to the movies or meet with friends for lunch or shoot pool at a local billiards hall instead of checking each job site, and the workers, daily. Some customers did not pay us for incomplete or shoddy work, so the workers were not paid in those cases. And when the workers were told again what they had to do in their jobs, or they would be fired, they upped and quit without notice.

My brother's youthful mistakes cost us some money. But we had learned a truly valuable lesson from that turn of events: the requirement that owners and managers must always be hands-on supervisors. We also realized that we must do so for the rest of our business lives.

We had no pickup trucks to transport our own lawn mowers either locally or to out of town sites. We could not finish the customers' lawns outside the area we initially covered ourselves. In two weeks, you can guess who took away most of our business from those "outside our local area" customers... the two workers who had quit. It was a disappointing lesson that we learned, but an important one. You absolutely have to follow your Business Plan 100% of the time or suffer the consequences. And you must ALWAYS oversee your business. The alternative is FAILURE. Fail to oversee your business and soon enough you won't have a business anymore to oversee.

Of course, being teens, we were too young and inexperienced at that time to know any better. But we learned from this situation that you have to make the time, have a firm commitment, and be a "Jack of all Trades" to run a successful business. We needed a clear definition of our business goal, products and service responsibilities. We had to pay attention to our customers, as the primary purpose for our business existence. We had to look ahead for a Business Plan on what our business should accomplish in those areas of growth, profitability, research and development, as well as facilities and organization. And we had to keep an eye on all facets of our business, including the workers and the job sites.

The moral of the story is you have to pay 100% of your time and attention to your own business or it will fail. 99% is not enough. My cousin learned from this experience, too! He and his dad later started up a manufacturing company. Years later, it grew so profitable that he sold it to a public company and retired. He got bored being retired and became a Gentleman Host on several passenger vacation boat lines to keep busy by ballroom dancing with guests. We still keep in touch with each other as good friends, to this date. And he always paid attention to the business he and his father founded - and was rewarded with success.

So, what makes Small Business owners successful? We all search for the secret of success in business. Some for money, some for power, and some for 101 other multi-faceted reasons.

You probably ask yourself how do you determine what makes a successful entrepreneur? They work long hours. They need strong moral support from their families and friends. They LOVE pressure, in fact they thrive on it. They are passionate about their work. They are methodical and organized. They are motivated to succeed. They are fiercely independent thinkers and actors. They create and work from a well- defined Business Plan. They value the success and the related prestige from being successful over the money rewards of the job, which they view less as a reward to the successful entrepreneur and more like a trophy. Money to a successful entrepreneur is more of a method to "mark" or rank (like in Monopoly) how successful you have become. It is more of a measure than an end. (But it still spends.)

Entrepreneurs are usually married, and have highly supportive spouses. They will do anything they have to do to succeed, except that which is against their moral values. Entrepreneurs are very honorable and most do business on a handshake – and they keep their word. A promise is a promise, whether it is written or not. And most of all, one thing stands out above all else, they want to succeed. No, strike that. They NEED to succeed. This drive to win is what they enjoy doing, and they must both enjoy what they are doing and be well versed in their field, in order to succeed.

Don't worry if you don't fit all of these qualifications: drive, organizational skills and work ethic can be acquired and used for success. Only the motivation and the spirit must already be there.

So let's remember **Mr. PHIL** (**M**arketable Idea, **R**ealistic Financials, Business **P**lan, **H**ard **I**ntense Work, **L**uck) as we introduce another concept to our ever-growing list of important terms to remember when starting a business: the 4 Stages of Entrepreneurship, or **SEAM**:

Startups, **E**arly Growth, **A**ccelerated Growth and **M**aturity.

Startups have the highest risk of failure. 80% of all new businesses fail or simply close or go out of business during their first 5 years. In fact, nearly seventy percent (70%) fail within 18 months. Why? The single most important factor is the lack of a solid and viable Business Plan, although the next highest reason for failure is related to insufficient capitalization (which will be covered in a later chapter). That means an entrepreneur must have total dedication to their business plan. This means that the entrepreneur will have to work long hours, cope with stress, and must have a viable and clearly defined set of goals. As a startup entrepreneur, you have to have adequate money for seed capital and expenses, customers and orders, plus the (absolutely critical) unconditional support of your family.

Early Growth requires brainstorming and a futuristic approach to attain your goal. Properly trained and knowledgeable staff is needed. Most important is a good marketing strategy for profitable sales.

Accelerated Growth will probably require more capital and additional credit facilities, which is the hardest thing to obtain. Second and Third stage funding is much harder to acquire because while the business may have a sales and growth track record, it is probably not yet profitable. **This is also the one thing not teachable or learnable from a book**. But some other keys are learnable. Like learning that if you have additional staff, you need to encourage individual team members to think about how to problem-solve for your company. As you grow, the key will be found when the most interesting questions are asked like when I talked at a Native American Community College in Minnesota. Most of the attendees, whether young or old, were lower middle-class families with a deep desire to get answers on how to succeed.

Additional financing at **Maturity** is necessary when you have to start to trim costs, stabilize the business operations and maintain a top, supportive staff. This is usually the stage where growth tapers off and the business needs funds for expansion or to replace aging equipment.

Many people ask their friends how they became so successful. It is a question that we ask of others. That prompted me to make a study of why people are successful in what they do. The answers proved interesting and I'd like to share some of those answers with you.

Entrepreneurs do not become successful because of money alone. Successful people are intense in their drive to succeed. All entrepreneurs work hard and long hours. They play hard, too. All of them care about what they do. They enjoy their work with a passion. Their attention span is short, but each person excels in what he or she does. They know their business, inside out, to the minutest details. And while they want to earn the money, **they don't do it for the money.**

Most successful entrepreneurs strive for perfection. Amazingly, each one I spoke to was positive in virtually everything they say or do. Practically all the people delivered more than was expected of them. Almost without exception, they have a winning smile that irresistibly charms you. And to the person, practically each one truly likes to deal with people. And they do it.

I met two people who especially fit that criterion. They operated a successful family restaurant. Their food was served buffet style, with huge trays of delicacies set out on a long counter. Dishes ranged from duck in cherry sauce to veal scaloppini, to curried shrimp, and succulent roast beef. Special cheese assortments were served before and during dinner. They were successful because they did the unusual-uncommonly well.

The owners greeted their customers with a gusto and enthusiasm that whetted one's appetites and made one feel like a very important person. Each platter had an exciting aura about it; each perfected and served with a story of its own. You felt you were truly dining, instead of just eating dinner out. In essence, success is simply selling yourself as a caring and concerned business person. It means giving that extra effort that many people overlook or take for granted. <u>It means believing in your business</u>.

You could say it is like a follow-up to "thank you for the order," after receiving it. A personal touch lets you care about them and their business. People caring about people and letting them know it is the key to lead to success. It is that extra care of service, material or product inspection before it is delivered, to make sure your customer is satisfied that makes the real difference in what a successful person does, and what makes a successful business, rather than just being another order taker. That is the difference when you're earning loyalty: long-term relationships in small business go with loyalty; customers love when businesses give them personal service, recognition, and care. The personal touch is the strongest bond between a business and a customer, and breeds loyalty in ways price or product does not.

And while we are talking about restaurants or any small business, how do you control against potential losses in your own business? Maybe you should be looking in the right places. Like most businesses, there are many problems running a restaurant business, for both solo Mom and Pop restaurants or for a chain or group. Great disparities exist due to the size of operations. All kinds of operating concerns are compounded in this ever-changing industry. And a majority of restaurants fail, due to high costs, poor service, or bad reviews. All contribute to losing customers.

But how to get and keep customers is not the only problem. What foods and price ranges do you need to specialize in for customer satisfaction?

What kind of portion controls should you have? What do you do with food not used (not leftovers, but unused or pre-cooked but unserved) from the day's sales? Then what about your labor, and the balance of wait staff and kitchen personnel, and what to do when someone fails to show up for work at the last minute? Then is the planning of menus, and forecasting of your food purchases. You need to purchase the best priced food products but also of sufficient quality. And making sure there's enough of what you need, from food to napkins to trash bags to clean tablecloths. All of this, plus pricing your menus to charge enough to make a profit but not too much to drive away customers are all part of the small business decisioning process.

When the speaker at a conference was asked "What is the one biggest problem you face in running your restaurant chain?" the answer was similar, yet unique. "We dump some of our garbage cans outside, near the end of the day, to see what was thrown out" (and how much) he said. "It helps us judge the quality of the vegetables and fruits delivered by suppliers to our various restaurant locations. We see how many broken plates, soup bowls, glasses, salt and pepper shakers, knives, forks and spoons were discarded." (This helps reduce shrinkage and waste.) We even found evidence of shrinkage in neatly wrapped, uncooked steaks and other products for someone to take (steal) home after working hours," he said. "Naturally, we had to make fast changes to correct these issues."

It was an eye opener. That lecture saved my own steel storage manufacturing company a lot of money in the future. We checked our scrap containers in our own business to see what good and bad product materials were thrown out and why? In the future, doing this inspection saved us a lot of money, too. Not only did we not scrap otherwise useful product, but we made sure the scrap dealers were honest about weights by estimating ourselves (using our own rough scale) how much we were scrapping.

The restaurant industry is growing at a record pace. These small businesses must keep up on pricing, rising costs in energy, and certain food products. Keeping an eye on volume buying discounts is a must. So while trends are changing rapidly for food and table service restaurants with more salads, wraps and ethnic foods (people are more adventurous in food selections) the bottom line is still the same.

Smart restaurateurs network with each other, to solve mutual problems (just like in other industries) and to build friendships with non-competing owners outside their market area. They do this to make friendships, and to exchange questions and answers about mutual issues or problems so they can find recommended solutions and advice.

It certainly gave us a lot to think about for our own future businesses.

So to sum up, to be a successful business person, you must work at it, regardless of the industry or product. 100 percent of the time, not less. It takes long practice and hard work. You have to believe in people and more important, you have to believe in yourself. To be like a real winner in business it will produce positive results for all small businesses, regardless of the product or service you are in. And you still need **Mr. PHIL**.

Remember that when you go to CHAPTER 3.

CHAPTER THREE
How To Start A Deal

Mr. PHIL is the **M**arketable Idea, the **R**ealistic Financials, the Business **P**lan, **H**ard **I**ntense Work, and *Luck.*

The most important part of the equation is the **P**. The **PLAN**. You need to know where you're going and how you're going to get there.

When I was in law school, I read some wonderful stories about Supreme Court Justice Oliver Wendell Holmes. There is one particular story that has stayed with me.

Justice Holmes was on a train going home and the conductor came along to ask him for his train ticket. Justice Holmes searched all his pockets, but he could not find his ticket. "Don't worry about it," said the conductor. "We know who you are, Justice Holmes."

"I'm glad you know me," he replied. "I am worried about that ticket, because it has my destination printed on it. Until I find it, I don't know where I am going."

Some people say that if you don't know where you are going, you will never get there. In fact, we all need to think where we want to go, if we want to fulfill our own dreams. Men and women who want to start their own small business or expand their existing one, have to ask themselves where they want their business to end up, what they have to do to get the business from where it is, to where they want it to be. Sometimes that means the owner will have to invest in more education, to get the training and the skills that are necessary to advance the business. It might mean getting more space to operate in, hiring key personnel or looking for additional financial aid - just plain money. But it all starts with a Plan.

We all need a road map to success. Think about how you plan a trip from one place to another because if you are like most of us, you get a road map layout or a hand-held cell phone and look at the route to highlight the one you take from start to finish, to get to your destination.

The business plan is a roadmap to how your business will operate and where it will go.

Generation-Y Millennials (born 1980-1994) and Gen-Z's (1995-2012) are the young men and women who today worry about attaining their realistic dreams for the future. Most want to be able to start a small business one day, from experiences learned working in their job. Most also realize they may never have it as good as their parents. But that doesn't mean they shouldn't try.

Generation Y for example, now between the ages of 26 to 40, have moved from education to full time employment, either on a temporary, part or full -time basis. They are growing up in a different world than past generations. They and their younger Gen-Z counterparts are living in a society which has moved from Television to Cable to Streaming, from rotary to touchtone to cellular phones, from dial up to 5G hyper-speed internet, and from newspapers and magazines to social media as their news source of choice. It not just radios anymore, now it's iTunes, Spotify, Pandora and Sirius XM.

Many young people today are well educated, team players and adaptable to change. In the past, a number of Generation X (1965-1979) workers changed jobs up to 6 times. Today, skills needed in work positions are different, but learnable, so Generations Y & Z will need guidance for future employment, financial security, job stability and career satisfaction, before they can start up a business of their own.

The answer is to stay in the field you like, become knowledgeable in it and choose a specific goal for the long term. Most skills can be learned on the job, whether you are a high school dropout, high school graduate or a graduate with a college degree.

Many first-generation Americans who could not find employment started their own business from humble beginnings. Most did not have a high school degree, but they had a hard work drive. They survived by working long hours and focusing on what they did best, with a passion to succeed. The present cohort must do that too, when they consider going into their own business.

I remember the story of my boyhood friend's father who was at the time a 15 year- old immigrant from Italy, who could not get a job, so to earn money he started to collect trash cardboard and rags in his local neighborhood. He collected the trash in 4 wheeled push carts. He learned where the cardboard trash went, the prices paid per pound and how the cardboard was eventually processed. His goal was to one day start a small cardboard processing plant of his own, which he did. He had determination to succeed, at the thing he knew best. It was his dream that grew into a multi-million dollars business.

I knew another young man who collected coins and paper money currency as a hobby. While he was waiting for a job opening, he started to sell to other collectors the $10 and $20- dollar bills that had numbers ending with four or five zeros, earning profits from it. He started to buy blocks of bills from various banks and continued to resell that specific currency to others. That hobby led to sales of coins on line, to collectors through the Internet. At 24 years of age, he had his own Small Business that earned a good living for him. There are hundreds, even thousands, of different ideas like those, for products and services you can consider when you go into your own small business.

Small business offers a leadership path for women, too! Most women starting in Small Business came up the ladder the hard way by working long hours and building upward-mobility contacts. Some women, out of work or semi-retired, sacrificed relationships because their mates would not relocate with them.

Women business leaders are aggressive in networking and meeting people, with a strong desire to carefully plan for their future. They have a drive in themselves to accomplish even the smallest tasks necessary, in order to succeed at what they do.

Both men and women learn valuable lessons about the advantages of networking. Even those really successful women were giving their calling cards out almost as fast as they could, in hopes of making contacts, that might help them in the future or to get to know other successful people to whom they could turn for advice, if they ran into problems.

To get an idea of various positions held in the 6800 (or so) worldwide women membership of the International Women's Forum (IWF), they are politicians, bank presidents, former state attorney generals, professional women in all fields, as well as presidents of small and big businesses. There is great opportunity in these economic times, to have a green light at the end of the road to glow and grow for women in small businesses.

Why not think out of the box! Let's take a business like food catering. Easy to learn. Easy to start. You get the business plan done and follow it like a road map. It takes only a few thousand dollars of seed money to get started. There are hundreds of businesses like it.

Or how about establishing an aqua-cultural farming small business in your region. If you grow enough fish for your business, you might be able to start a flash freeze processing plant to include the adjoining region's businesses to supply their excess fish for processing. This is another type "home based" business that could be partnered with food market chains or individual venture capitalists.

How about a "silk screen and embroider small business" for shirts and clothing merchandise to be sold on the internet or direct to large corporation buyers?

The end results are only a few of the hundreds of innovative ways to get into various businesses and work hard to succeed.

- - - -

My friends called me "BF" from my early startup small business days. It all started when my soon-to-be-wife Sandra phoned my office and wanted to speak to her "BF". She meant "Boy Friend", but it was thought to be an "in thing" with our office staff and suppliers, so everyone called me "BF" from that time on, until I became Mayor of Highland Beach, Florida in 2011. Thereafter, I became known as either "Your Honor or Mayor Featherman." I actually grew out of the name "BF" as I grew better known in the community. I'm now "Mr. Mayor."

Sandra and I met at a downtown party in Philadelphia. She had just graduated from the University of Pennsylvania. She caught my eye - so carefree and full of life. We talked together almost the whole night. I remember calling her "my little lost waif," when we first talked. I tried to get her to go out for dinner on either of the next two nights, but she had dates for each day, so I asked her to go out to lunch with me the next day and she said yes. That was the positive selling point for me!

When I came to her house for the first time, and said hello, I kissed her. She told me several months afterwards, she said to her mother that she had fallen in love at first sight with me, and she would never see me again except through rose-colored glasses. She told her mother she was going to marry me one day and sure enough, she did the following year. It was the best non-business plan I've ever gone into, with no formal plan to do so. And it enriched me handsomely for a lifetime!

Sandra stuck to the education field, but also became an outstanding community activist, as well. She became what I would call the "intrapreneur" of the family. She rose through the ranks of academia to reach a vice presidential level at a Midwestern university, and then became the president of the University of New England for 11 years. Meanwhile, in the "community" aspect of her life, she had become a lifetime trustee of one major charitable foundation while also serving as a member, trustee, or board member of literally dozens of other charitable and non-profit boards, as well as a number of business organizations. She, like me, is listed in both the Marquis "Who's Who in America" and "Who's Who in the World" – the "real" ones.

Sandra and I learned a lot from our volunteer involvement in the various profit and non-profit organizations we joined. They would have been helpful in my failed lawn mowing business; had we followed the proper and required business procedures in our Business Plan 100% of the time, we would have succeeded. Just like our foray into steel tubing, where the employees taught me about dealing with staff and employees of companies and concerns affecting their jobs.

So I was in my early 20's, and it was time to get experience in the retail trade, something that would greatly affect my future choices. I started a summer job with a local industrial equipment company. The owner was a middle-aged man who talked loud to us, worked us hard on the job, and seemed to do a lot of business on a cash basis. I liked him because he was a matter of fact, honest guy, who told the straight-out truth to everyone. His company dealt mainly in used steel shelving, office equipment and odd lots of used material handling equipment. The foreman and I usually loaded and unloaded surplus shelving and material handling equipment goods off or on the owner's small truck, in addition to various commercial freight trucks.

We stacked and packed the loose, used shelving parts into strapped packages. Sometimes the shelving and material handling equipment were repainted or cleaned by hand, to be presentable for resale. The owner purchased used or surplus steel equipment from private companies, at auctions or companies going out of business.

My first five weeks on the job left me both mentally and physically aching from lifting heavy bundles and packages, some weighting over 50 pounds. I worked 5 days a week, from 6:30 am in the morning to around 6:00 pm, and even sometimes on Saturdays, for $10 pay a week. I felt I should have been compensated at least $2 more a week, for the work done. I went into the bosses' office and asked for a $2 raise. He said NO, he could not afford it since he paid his foremen only $12 a day. So, I gave him notice and I quit the job the next week.

One day as I was coming home from classes at college I bumped into my former employer, at a subway stop in town. He told me he recently had gone bankrupt and was having a hard time paying any bills.

I told him that a person contacted me about a week ago, who had five truckloads of used shelving to sell. He asked me if I was interested to buy or sell it, or did I know someone who could sell it in partnership with him? He left his name and phone number which I gave to my former old boss, so maybe he could work out a deal with that person.

Two months later, my old boss called me at home to let me know he went into partnership on the deal, he as the seller, and the other person as the investor. He sold the entire lot of shelving to one of his largest customers and made enough money to get back into his old used shelving business. He never forgot that favor I did for him. It reinforced my views on personal satisfaction in in helping others in time of need. Years later, he kept his promise to buy new shelving or other equipment from whatever company I was associated with.

These were experiences that I had to gain myself by working, not through teaching. I learned about working personnel concerns, business conditions, and responsibilities to customers, that would stay with me for the rest of my life.

Because of these and other events, I was beginning to question what time is worth, for services and goods rendered. Is it the markup to charge on hours of actual time spent on work done or was it to be based on the total savings outcome to the customer? In other words, a flat rate for the job or an hourly rate on the work that was done. Each decision may be correct, depending on the situation and agreements to be entered into by both parties.

I read somewhere about a manufacturer that was running considerably below capacity, due to an undetermined machine problem. Something was wrong but their experienced yet confounded staff could not find out what. An expert was called in to help, and when he arrived, he put on work clothes, grabbed some note pads from his bag, and proceeded to walk around the entire facility, checking out all of the plant's equipment. The second day, he took out a can of red spray paint, and painted a giant "X" on the side of a machine on the floor. "This machine is the source of the problem. Replace this machine with a new working one and your production will return to normal." Then he left. No one else had seen the small error in the defective machine's design but the expert. The machine was creating defective parts in the production chain, and was replaced with a new, proper one, within a week. Now, all of a sudden, things started being made properly again, and production returned to normal. The problem was solved; the expert had done their job.

One week later, an invoice arrived for $5,000. A steep price for just the two days of work. The plant manager, who was responsible for approving and paying the invoice, wanted to know how the expert justified their price, so he asked him to justify his bill and "break down" the invoice. A few days later, the expert's revised bill arrived. It read "Red 'X' painted on defective machine, $5.00. Consultant's Fee for knowing which machine to paint with the Red 'X', $4995.00. Total Price, $5,000.00." Expertise, service, and time. How simple that is and yet so difficult for some to understand. When your service results in the solution to your customer's problem, you have done your job, and earned your payment. How many times have you short changed yourself for the services you perform? This story shows that both a person's time and knowledge is worthy of compensation for their services.

To keep a customer, you must bill fairly, of course. Maybe $10,000 was the going rate for the expert's "fix" or maybe it was excessive. That's not the point. The idea is to be socially responsible, to be honorable in all that you do. You should operate with complete integrity, whether it is for one dollar or ten thousand dollars. Small businesses that sell services rather than products must set similar rules for dealing with similar service circumstances. But let's get back to what we did in our earlier years to make money.

We went back to the streets again for business. We stenciled street numbers on the curbs in front of row houses in the city. We went in the evening hours to each home to ask for a minimum contribution of 50 cents for the stenciling of their street address on the curb in front of their house. Some gave, some didn't. We averaged about $20 a day for a 50/50 split between us. To make even more money, we ran errands for neighbors who were too busy, old or sick to get certain things done. We picked up and delivered groceries, returned books to the library, picked up and deliver clothing from the dry cleaners. And that's not all. That was the start of a small business by two young entrepreneurial teenagers. We were creating business where it did not exist before. It's a challenge to be your own boss; to make your own money without working under someone else's control. It was a driving force to constantly start another and another new business, especially when you get tired of running one you are currently running. We were on a roll again. (Must be fattening, all these rolls…)

We liked new things, new adventures, and meeting new people as we moved from one venture to another. We got tired of doing the same thing over and over, when we were already starting to make money. That's when the feeling comes; the one that "it's now time to look around for a new business venture" – a new, different way to make more money. For two young teenagers it was a constant learning mode.

My other brother and I talked about making a line of steel table slides, used under kitchen and dinette tables. The idea came to us when he noticed the big, wooden table slides underneath the dining room table tops, used to expand or close down the length of the table top. Wood slides seemed big and bulky, heavy in weight and probably more expensive in shipment costs from the manufacturer. We decided to investigate it right away to see if it could be a viable product.

During a time-study night course I took during my MBA studies I learned you could save time by combining functions. Like, for example, stamping two rivets in place at one time instead of separately. This let us assemble two pieces of steel into one complete slide unit from two blanks of steel, but in one step. With lighter gauge steel, we could make it efficiently and quicker. The steel slides were designed by my younger brother, who graduated from college with an industrial engineering degree. The steel slides were much lighter in weight than the heavier,

48

bulky wood slides sold by our competitors. Our steel slides would both save assemblers time to install, and result in lower freight costs. We determined that we could make the stampings and assemble the slides in our father's vacant 8000 sq. foot building at no rental charge, provided we took care of the maintenance costs and responsibilities for the building. He left us two old press brakes, several punch presses, tooling and dies, and a tubing pipe bending machine, all from a former steel bed manufacturing business that he mothballed a few years earlier. He told us we could use all the old machinery to make the steel table slides. Now, we could get into another business and no added machinery costs would be necessary nor any rental charges for the facility space.

We drew up a Business Plan to outline what our costs were to make the table slides, how we would manufacture and market them, at what price we should sell them, the estimated profit to be made, the market merchandising area to sell, the factory and office personnel we would need to produce the product and the sales, the amount of money we would need to cover overhead, and the financing that we would need for the business to make it all work.

So, what we did is we made up one-page mailers in five different colors, to solicit companies in the Yellow Pages phonebook that were listed as manufacturers of dinette and kitchen tables, to try our metal table slides. We mailed a different colored mailer to them each month, and then took turns phoning each prospective customer to personally promote our product and to offer them a few free samples of our table slides, at no charge, to get them to try our product in the belief that if they tried it, they would like it enough to buy. The multicolored mailers and samples we provided were paying off for us. Orders for samples slide units started to come, and so did a lot of regular paid orders.

Some manufacturers making high priced dining tables wanted to use only wood slides, but many small business dinette assemblers were interested in trying out our steel table slides, as they were cheaper in price to the assembler, and could be provided to them quickly. I borrowed a car and took drives as far as a hundred or more miles away to visit regional assemblers and manufacturers of dinette tables, to hunt for customers. Sales were starting to come in, and we were selling more than 3000 sets a month.

We researched the table slide business used in the industry. We reviewed potential sales and profits. We studied the wood competition. We knew where to buy the steel blanks, cut to size, from a local steel distributor. After production started, we could shop around for other competitive sources with better prices. Our seed capital, a family loan, provided us enough cash to last for nine months while we grew the business. Since we three brothers were young and unmarried at the time, we didn't have to worry about the huge financial burden of supporting a family, and this allowed us to run lean and mean.

We chose to form a Partnership, which eased the burden of taxes. We rehired some of the former workers from the bedding business to do the stamping, bending, and riveting of the table slide parts together, which gave us good, older, experienced workers who showed up on time and gave us an honest day's work for a day's pay. We were able to get open credit on steel materials bought and backed by a small line of credit at a local bank that was familiar with and friendly to our father and his former company, and trusted from our name and reputation that we would repay them.

The big users of steel table slides were the smaller Dinette kitchen assemblers. They were interested because the steel table slides were cheaper in price, deliveries were faster, and freight charges were lower. We sold the slides for $2.50 per set in lots of 500 units or more. Anything less than that quantity was $3.00 per set. Our cost to make the slides were .62 cents per set. Orders and profits built up over 18 months and then two metal stamping competitors started to sell our customers for 10% less than our price. As an early adopter, we had a jump on the industry, but as deeper pockets come in and undercut us, we started to lose business. This pattern was not unique to our business; every business type suffers the same problem. So, we had a problem, and in order to compete and stay in business, we reduced our sales prices several times over the next year. First to $1.75, then to $1.50 cents, later to $1.25 cents per set, and finally we lowered the price to $.99 cents per pair, to undercut both competitors. That is when they dropped out of the market and we reclaimed our customers all to ourselves. Now we could start to expand our sales, and we did, to market and sell to customers in the midwest of the country.

We then revisited idea we had been talking about for almost 6 months. Why not partner with a supplier of upholstered seating and table top manufacturer? Three partners to make better and more profitable products. The deal was settled that we would assemble the complete dinette package, include supplying table slides and steel tubing at our cost plus 20% for overhead. We would fabricate the tubing chair frames. The seating parts would be supplied by one partner while the other partner would supply the table tops through the same arrangement. Steel was still on allocation (this meant some shortage of supply occurred) but one of our uncles made sure we could get enough steel tubing for our chair production. We started to assemble the entire dinette sets in our factory, and we made direct shipments to the resale dealer trade. The idea was viable, and potentially profitable.

The two suppliers would each be one-third partners along with us in the venture. I learned a lot of things going around trade shows and through in-person visits to companies; one of those things was that many companies will consider joining a partnership if you keep that fact confidential AND you show them how that partnership will make them money while not conflicting with their existing business. I found several companies that were interested in joining with us, but hit "pay dirt" when I chose two different non-competing of suppliers to finally partner with us in the deal.

"PDC" was formed, with the three companies, ourselves and our two partners, each owning an equal share of the company and splitting the profit three equal ways. The new venture started just two months later. Our table top partner even brought in a CPA firm to do our accounting services (this solved another problem) that had handled several other dinette assembler accounts, so we acquired a knowledgeable source of information to run our business that provided solutions in the future.

The end result was that we had means to produce our product, shared risk, costs and financing, and diversity in both manufacture and customer bases. This only helped us on our quest to be successful. And as a bonus, our partners were supplying two-thirds of the material. Our business started as an idea, and grew into a small business, which then grew into a larger one.

All from an idea. And a Plan.

Which brings up "The Question" of "Can I Be Successful, And What Will It Take?" To be successful as an entrepreneur, you need to have more than drive. You have to have a Plan. And know answers to the following...

KEY QUESTIONS TO ASK YOURSELF AS A BUDDING FUTURE ENTREPRENEUR

1. Is my knowledge and business experience adequate for the business I want to enter?

2. Can I take full responsibility?

3. Can I organize for myself and for others?

4. Will I commit to work the necessary long hours daily, or on weekends?

5. Will I stay, in the face of any or all adverse situations I may face, and not quit?

6. Can I prepare a proper and adequate BUSINESS PLAN that covers the first 3-5 years?

7. Can I survive for up to the first 18 months without taking a salary, so I do not waste seed capital?

8. Can I state my mission and goals simply?

9. Do I have access to good professionals like CPAs, lawyers, insurance brokers and others?

10. Will my family support my plans and stand behind me?

11. How is my health?

12. Is this what I really want, and will I stick with it?

And then there is the Plan.

A business plan is a blueprint that takes you from an idea or concept to an actual brick-and-mortar running business. (Or, a web business, but this book is about the concept, not the type, of business.)

The (SAMPLE) BUSINESS PLAN

The following is a (very) brief outline of a business plan, which will be expanded on later in the book.

Business Statement. This is a short 1-2-page statement about what the business is, how it expects to succeed, why it expects to succeed, and, most importantly, why it deserves investor money.

Executive Summary. This is an outline of the key parts of your plan. The purposes are to attract Investors and set out the ideology of the business. Two to three pages long at most, it must avoid fancy terms, wild claims, and unnecessary charts (unless critical to the business) so that credibility is maintained.

Company Description. This is straightforward. What type of business? Merchandising? Manufacturing? Service? What's the current status: start up, expansion or takeover? It is a sole proprietor, partnership, or corporation? Why should an investor believe the business will be profitable?

Market Analysis. This includes product definition, trade area, market sales volume, potential or current customers, competition, and what will be the keys to success such as location, price, and quality.

Product and Services. This tells your products or services, states your value to the consumer, compares competing products or services, summarizes production costs and identifies your intellectual property.

Marketing and Sales. How will you sell your product or service? This covers target market-geographic/ industry/type of buyer, pricing strategy and distribution.

Operations. The details of how the business produces the products or services it sells. It covers Plant (physical facility, location, size, how configured), Material and Machinery (what machinery, leased or purchased), Labor (how many workers, what type, what pay) and Administration (office and sales costs).

Management and Ownership. Who will be running the business, and why.

Organization and Personnel? Who works there? Your staff, organizational chart, and responsibilities. This is important to show: Who does what? Who reports to whom? How is management paid?

What skills or training is required? Full or part time employees? How much are people paid?

Funds Required and Uses. (This is one of the two most important parts to investors, along with Business Summary.) First and foremost, how much money is being requested for how much required, and what does an investor get for their investment (if an investor-focused Plan)? How will the money be spent? (i.e. working capital, new equipment, inventory, supplies, etc.) Who are the suppliers? How approves expenditures, and is there a check-and-balance system in place?

Financial Data. This is straightforward. Financials both historical (if applicable) and forward-projecting. These include a proforma balance sheet, a P&L or profit and loss statement, a cash-flow statement, and comparative financials or industry ratios regarding competitors or the industry group at large.

Finally, Other. This is where other matters are addressed, like contracts, documents, NDA agreements or employment requirements, and such. (This section is not always included.)

This BUSINESS PLAN applies to all new business startups and is the most essential part of a new business other than the initial financing.

And now, let's go to Chapter 4. The Business Plan.

CHAPTER FOUR
The Business Plan

John Donne once said "No man is an Island, entire of itself; every man is a piece of the continent, a part of the main…" It was true almost four centuries ago. It is even more so in the business world today. We are all interdependent: dependent on each other and all other segments of our industry for our mutual survival - and to thrive.

Almost everybody dreams of getting rich one day from being a successful businessman or woman. The fact is most of us work just to get enough money to pay our monthly bills, with little left over.

Small business owners must think differently than the average person to become wealthy. It means breaking out of the mindset learned in early childhood, in order to make that dream come true today.

From early youth, we are brought up to focus on education: get good grades, attend classes on time, do what we are told. In other words, follow the rules for the things that prepare us for the job world we enter when we graduate. Yet, similar to a cookie cutter syndrome, everybody does not have to be like everyone else. Small business people not only have to be driven, but frugal and self-sacrificing. One must revise their way of thinking and break out of the cookie-cutter mold; try something beyond our present capabilities by doing new things that are non-traditional way, not done before by the dreamer.

Some of us have heard the story of the baby elephant, chained by its rear leg to a stake in the ground. The baby elephant was not strong enough to pull up the stake holding it down from moving about. Even after growing to adulthood, the elephant's mindset prevented it from pulling the stake out of the ground. That became a control mechanism on the elephant's mind the rest of its adult life, as changing one's mind set and learning new ways is easy to say, but hard to do.

Just like in school, we work in business by adhering to its rules and regulations. We don't make waves. We look for recognition. We are team players and loyal to our company. In return, we get good wages and future promotions. But what do we do when our company's business fortunes are reversed, affected by a down turn in the economy and employee layoffs occur?

Whether you are in your twenties or over 50 years of age, many employees are laid off from their jobs and it may include you or a family member. Sounds familiar? That's the time to consider your dreams to reinvent yourself, by starting your own small business.

Put your dream to work by galvanizing your ideas into action. Niche yourself into the knowledge you already have. After working for others, change directions in your life so you can make things happen. When you feel you have the necessary skills and talent, start your dream by going into a small business. Just remember the elephant story and start to think the "I can do." It is your incentive to change your thinking from the past, to the present time.

Look for a product or service that is needed in your community. Start learning about it and stay with it. Perseverance, determination, knowledge of your products and passion to sell it, can make your dream come true. Think **Mr. PHIL** and make it work for you.

Change your pre-programming from "No can do" to "We can do." Successful small business owners think that way. They are action people who enjoy what they do and make money doing it at the same time. They walk the talk, learning from their past successes as well as past failures. They are achievers and positive minded people who believe in them. You can be a person of any age, with a dream one day to go into a startup small business and succeed.

My own father, who ran a small business, said many times "always plan ahead on everything you do." Those were wise words that I still follow today, in both business and private life. During my graduate MBA studies at Temple University, I learned the importance of what those words meant for a successful business venture by planning ahead, with a Business Plan. You have to stay true to your own vision by planning what to do and how to do it.

Most start-up small businesses change their plans and operations multiple times, with some being major changes. This requires the ability to modulate the business plan and change quickly without destroying the overall plan. While a full-blown plan that covers three to (preferably) five years forward, there should also be a short-term plan that can be amended on the fly. Plans for less than three years are not long-range enough to address major contingencies, or raise capital. Big businesses make continuing 5-10 year forward projected plans. Short plans such as one or two years in length do not address rapid economic or market changes, and are unproductive for long range planning.

Yet to start-up a small business, it's hard to plan too far in advance. Things are too dependent on the whims of the market. Sudden shortages or gluts in material or even services are altered worldwide with frightening, unexpected speed. Yesterday's great buys could be today's disasters, and shocks to your industry or geographical area can easily harm the market for your services or goods to be sold.

Small businesses regularly encounter staffing and supply problems, sales troubles, and financial problems; all have to be solved, and quickly. They have to be dealt with depending on the whims of the marketplace, money, governmental laws and product changes that must be corrected, if the business is to survive. Owners typically have good business instincts (some call it a "nose" for what's happening in their industry) but they still have to refine their projections and "guesses" and make make-or-break decisions about what they are looking for and looking at, where to go, and what to do to get there and once you "arrive" there. Successful planning requires taking specific indicators and projecting them into different time frames. For instance, sales decisions will depend on your near-term projections. Picture where you would be at an eight or twelve yearly market period, then craft a second -year projection of what you have to do internally to get there. Make your plan revisions, and then see if they make sense.

There is an ancient Chinese proverb that says "If you don't know where you are going, any road will get you there" and what that means is that you can take any path if you have no preference, and wherever you get to, you're there. Business Plans are no different. They can be slanted to appeal to different investors, bankers, venture capitalists, friends, family, whoever. No specific path needs to be in the plan; whatever your plan is, it is. It can be anything you want it to be, but with the caveat that if it isn't viable, it won't get you to where you want to go. If it does not make sense, and show how you will get from start-up to profit making and in a specific amount of time, no one will finance it and it will fail.

SO WHAT DO YOU NEED TO DO TO PREPARE FOR DRAFTING A BUSINESS PLAN?

1. Research the business or field you intend to go into

   A. Talk to those already in that business or service

   B. Go to the library and borrow (and read) business and finance books

   C. Contact trade associations, and maybe not just for your chosen field

   D. Subscribe to trade publications in the field appropriate for your new business

   E. Contact the US Small Business Association (SBA). They have dozens of publications on various businesses. I personally read over 12 publications in the last year.

   F. Where is the business to be located is important- LOCATION, LOCATION, LOCATION. Just like real estate, your geographic sales market is crucial to your success. Pick the right location to have a better chance.

2. Project sales and profits for the first three years; five to ten years is better. **And Be Realistic, Not Idyllic!**

3. Study the competition. If possible, go to work for a future competitor for a year and learn.

4. Create an image of your company. Create a logo, company colors, motto, letterhead, calling cards and brochures. Determine your predicted levels of service, quality and ads. Propose initial pricing for your service or product, and how you justify the price. Remember that price alone is not the only reason many customers might choose you over someone else.

5. You absolutely positively must have enough initial capital or financial reserves to survive – without any revenues – for at least 18 months. While you should expect your business to generate income quickly or in the first few months, you must have enough money for working capital and reserve funds that

assume no immediate income. And remember that bankers are neither your partners nor your friends and will not hesitate to foreclose and/or call your loan if they even suspect you might not be able to pay it back. So you must have ample initial funding to sustain your business should revenues or expenses not match what you proposed in your plan. Remember: while you may be able to start some businesses on a "shoestring" most require real money to grow enough to be sustainable.

6. Use professionals like consultants, a good lawyer, a top-notch accountant, and an insurance broker. Get a mentor. Ask your friends and colleagues, or retired business people in your field, or organizations like SCORE and SBDC, for advice and help. These are all good sources to keep in contact with, both to help you network, and to solve any of your business problems.

7. Know where to buy, what to buy, and how to buy to maximize your revenue and minimize your costs. Look for consignment deals, closeouts, and see if you can buy supplies on credit.

Our dinette business was running successfully. Our steel table slides business was not. The slides business had a declining return on profits due to new entrant competitors, who entered about two years after we did, who sold at lower prices than ours. Because of this, my brothers and I began planning to change our focus and looked at what other types of businesses we could go into. Maybe we could use the unused section of factory space still available to us. It contained metal fabricating equipment that had not been used for a few years, such as old punch presses, press brakes and a small paint line. They were still installed on the factory floor, and presumably still worked, or would, with a little restoration.

During our discussions, the used steel shelving story came up. I explained to my brothers what had happened during time on that job, and how only two weeks ago, while waiting for a trolley at the subway stop, I bumped into my old boss and told him about the five truckloads of used steel shelving that was offered to me. The offeror gave me his name and telephone number, just in case I knew of someone who might be interested in buying them from him. I then recounted how I had turned it down. The former boss then asked me if he could contact that man, since he told me he had gone into bankruptcy several months earlier and was looking for some kind of deal that could help him to make money again. I felt sorry for his situation, so I gave him the man's name and phone number who had the used steel shelving for sale. When my old boss called him, it turned out he became the seller on the deal; the man offering the 5 truckloads became the investor on the deal. Together, they sold the entire lot. My old boss made enough money on the deal to settle some past debts and go back into business again.

There are many options for doing a successful venture. A strong selling point for us to consider on going into the steel shelving fabrication business was that we already had a factory which was set up in such a way as to facilitate fabricating shelving. The used equipment was still there, in place, and available to us to use make a new product line like steel shelving. That there was remaining vacant space at the factory was the key in our giving it deep consideration. We agreed to take that careful consideration, and when we did, we realized that while the shelving business fascinated us enough to consider it, we needed significantly more information before we would go into a field we knew little about.

I thus agreed to get that information so we could make a decision. I began the research very seriously on what we needed to do. We had three months to find the data and evaluate before we had to decide yes or no. Steps had to be taken to prepare a Business Plan by identifying what our main objective would be. In this case, we decided that we would manufacture a limited product line of steel shelving for resale distribution. We drafted an Executive Summary and put it into a full-blown Business Plan. Once this was done, we could review the results at our next meeting.

First, to get information, I talked to my old boss at his office about the steel shelving market. He was very responsive because of the favor I had done for him that had effectively put him back in business. He was honest and truthful. In fact, he told me he placed several new steel shelving orders with a shelving manufacturer in New York, which he had arranged to be "drop-shipped" direct to his customer by the manufacturer. (A Drop-Shipment is where Company "Alpha" buys a product from Company "Beta" which Alpha then sells to their final customer or "end-user" Company "Charlie." The products are delivered by Beta to Charlie but have the Alpha on the products and on the paperwork so that the fact that Beta was the manufacturer is invisible to

Charlie and it appears that Alpha was the manufacturer.) While new shelving was only a small part of his retail business, it was a profitable one for him. And yes, he felt there was room for a local shelving supplier to make sales to dealers like him.

I spoke to a number of East Coast based resale distributors that all sold new steel shelving made by someone else. Their shelving sales were mainly drop-shipped by the manufacturers direct to the final customer but with the distributor's name as shipper. Some distributors also carried a full stock of steel shelving in their warehouses for customer pick up, mainly in the six primary industry sizes: depths of 12" 18" and 24" each in width sizes of 36"and 48" for a total of six sizes.

We worked out the individual shelving component breakdowns on material and labor costs for shelves and upright posts, including hardware and bolts and nuts for unit assembly, and paint and cartons costs. Our insurance company filled us in on the costs of both employee and product liability coverage. After reviewing these costs, and things like the utility and other miscellaneous overhead charges, and adding professional fees and costs, we then raised each expense by an additional 5% to cover any contingencies or other things we might have missed. This gave us a cost factor and an idea of what we would have to charge if we wanted to make a profit making and selling shelving to these distributors.

We got a lot of Yellow Page telephone books, and looked for the listings for resale shelving distributors and dealers in ten major cities. We used this list to generate call lists so we could for phone each resale shelving distributor and ask what they thought of their current shelving suppliers. (This would give us an idea as to whether there was an opening for us to enter the market.) Furthermore, a mailing list gleaned from this call list would prove useful to us so we could send out literature to these potential customers, and so we could make contact by phone or personal visits if we decided to start out shelving company. While they did not exist at the time, another possibility that is viable now is the use of text messages and social media advertising to help attract customers and get leads to give to our resale distributors.

We mailed to the Shelving Manufacturers Association for a list of all of their manufacturing members. We received it back by return mail and it was very useful for us to get competitive list prices and trade discounts.

Many years later, when our company became a major presence in the shelving industry, I had the distinct honor to serve as their[i] National President.

The U.S. Small Business Administration ("SBA") was contacted to get information for us on how to understand Small Business set-aside orders that were extended to small businesses, veterans and minority owned businesses by the government. We estimated that we would be small enough to qualify for this program. We learned about what help the SBA offered to assist small businesses in getting business from the federal government. We learned about this while talking to several small shelving distributors, and then learned more once we received responses back from the SBA. We also discovered a brochure published by the government that listed all types of items that were available for bidding by companies, bids we would be able to enter in order to have a chance to win a government contract to supply products to various government agencies. It included information on what agency to contact and the closing dates for respective bids to be submitted to each of them, and the terms and conditions.

I visited a few shelving manufacturers' plants and got their list prices on all the shelving products they supplied to consumers and industrial users, along with the distributor discounts that they offered to the trade. In some industries prices are fixed, but sometimes they vary. Also, in some industries there is a list price for sale to end users, but a discount schedule that applies to the dealer or distributor who arranges the sale. In the shelving industry, we discovered that almost all sales of new products were made through dealers or distributors who paid the manufacturer a discounted rate from the list price, and the list price was paid by the end user to the distributor, who always appeared as the seller. The lone exception is when sales are to a governmental entity (federal, state or local) which had to be sold to at the lowest price the manufacturer sells to any other lowest-price buyer. This is called "most favored nation" status and in most cases is required by law. In these situations, the manufacturer sells and bills directly, but pays a small commission to the dealer or distributor who represents the manufacturer in that geographic or industrial region.

Next, we met with family members and close friends to explore raising working capital for the first nine months of operations of our fledgling shelving business. We didn't get much. Family members are loath to lend money for speculative business investments, especially to other family members.

We then met with two bankers to explore short- and long-term loans, collateralized (guaranteed) by orders received from resale distributors (e.g., customer payments to us), as well as material needed by us to manufacture the shelving parts to distributors (inventory). The results were positive on the funding end to be received from these two bankers. Banks generally will lend to new businesses where they can secure the entire value of the loan. Typically, this is done through securing the inventory and receivables of the business. Sometimes the bank will wait for each month's payment from the company, and sometimes a new business will have to "lock-box" payments where all customer payments go to a Post Office Box and the bank deposits them directly and credits the company with excess over the amount due that month.

Some people have a hard time understanding why other Small Business people are successful. What they want to hear is a good luck story, or a gimmick to explain success rather than to believe the truth: that good planning and hard work is what is truly responsible for all of it.

My answer for success is deceptively simple. It has just two precepts: PRE-PLANNING and HARD WORK. You have to start with a business plan and then work hard to deliver the goods and services you identified in the plan. Reliability and dependability build businesses. Customers come to you and return to you for repeat orders only because they either have no other source, or they begin to believe that you honestly care about their business and their needs. You become trusted by your customers because you reflect integrity in your relationship with them, and always deliver what you promise to their business. And when you promise something, you must always deliver it.

Reputation means dependability for on-time deliveries, fair pricing, and, of course, keeping your word. Everything in life is a risk, but your word should be your bond. Trust is hard earned but easily lost.

One time I promised a sales representative (they work for themselves and represent you with respect to your line of goods or services) a commission on an important sale. He had done significant work to obtain the sale, spending his own time and money. Due to an issue no one could predict in advance, I had to cancel the order. Nonetheless, I promised the man a commission and, true to my word, and even though I paid for it myself out of my own pocket and not from company funds, I kept my promise and paid him the commission. This is one example of why whenever I did business and gave my handshake or promise, it was more binding – and trusted more – than a written contract. My word was (and still is) considered as valuable as gold in whatever I do because I do not go back on my word. You need to do the same if you want to be respected in your field and trusted by your contemporaries, employees, partners, and customers. Your word MUST be your bond. And you must always go out of your way to honor it, even at a personal cost, and no matter the cost.

Hard work is always the magic ingredient. The saying is "(Ninety percent perspiration and ten percent aspiration." It is that "90 percent perspiration" that makes successful people successful people. They put in the effort to succeed. I have sat up half the night, more nights than I want to remember, because I had work to get done. That means many nights I came home late to dinner because the order needed expediting, and I had to be there to expedite it. And as a small business owner, no problem was too small that didn't desire (or require) my personal attention, when I was informed about it.

My observation of most other successful small business people in life is that they work hard and put in the hours to get the job done. And done right, or not at all. And in business, there is no "not at all" or else there is no business.

I knew a fellow who wanted to be a Small Business owner one day. "But I'll only work from 8am to 4pm and take off weekends to travel and have fun and games, other than business," he told me. That was over five years ago. Nothing has changed in that time. I don't think he will ever run his own business, let alone be successful at it. You must be willing to do the hard work or you will never succeed.

Responsible small business owners care about their businesses, and both their - and their employees' - jobs. They care about doing things right. They worry about how customers and employees are treated. And they do their work with a passion. That's how they become successful. It's all in how they develop personal satisfaction in whatever they do that makes for success.

Times change, but the modus operandi of success remains the same. You owe it to yourself, your employees and customers to pre-plan well, to delegate properly and to set your goal high so you can achieve the success in life that you deserve. Many say the future is for the swiftest, for the tough minded and for the most innovative person. Maybe so, maybe no, but that's the way I would bet to win. You can too.

There is a leadership path in networking, for both men and women in startups of small businesses. Whether some men or women inherit substantial wealth, most people came up the ladder the hard way, working long hours and building upward mobility contacts. Many men or women sacrificed relationships because their mates would not relocate or work closer with them.

Both men and women learn a valuable lesson from the advantages of aggressive networking and meeting people, with a strong desire to carefully plan for their future. Successful small business people have a desire to accomplish even the smallest tasks necessary in order to succeed at what they do.

There are valuable lessons about the advantages of networking for a start-up small business. The most successful people give out their calling cards (or V-Cards in today's technological age; either works) as fast as they can, in hopes of making useful contacts that might help them in the future. Many small business people get to know other successful people to whom they could turn for advice as mentors, should they run into business problems.

One example was my wife's membership in the International Women's Form (IWF), which works to advance women as leaders by building a network among women of achievement. They share business, social, public, and political issues of mutual concern. The IWF has worldwide membership of about 6800 women who are presidents and CEO's of small and big businesses, bank and college presidents, judges, lawyers, political leaders in government and women leaders in every profession.

The place to start for leadership is to begin a small business and grow to succeed. That's my way to bet on it. I learned that in starting a business, you need to build good will; your company has to prove itself as ethical, responsible and trustworthy in dealing with new distributors and end user customers. Each business creates its own image. Sufficient working capital is necessary to ensure you don't run out of money for materials, salaries or operating expenses. You will need to make a sales projection for your first year in business, and to estimate what profits you require for future growth, staff and labor workers, management costs and working capital. It may be necessary to have a specific line of new products, bought from other manufacturers on a jobbed (resale) basis, to round out your line or to attract more distributors. That really means you will need additional financing to cover those increased sales.

The question to be resolved is where your company will sell your products or services now or in the future and what additional money will be needed to run your business, as you will have to forecast ahead of time on a growing or declining market. What determines your breakeven point is in actual sales that will determine the profits you can make in a business. One reason is estimated market sales to be reached by a specific time, the second reason is the cost to manufacture each product, which included other overhead expenses. All this, plus assets and future good will, including cash-flow, are the necessary parts of making a successful entrepreneur. An experienced CPA firm should be contacted, who can do this work for you at a very minimal charge.

My brothers and I realized our knowledge of the steel shelving market was uncertain and there were substantial risks, but it paid for us to start a shelving business so we would be our own bosses. With our positive attitudes, our potential to make money and grow really looked great. We also had each other - we had each other to "watch our backs" so to speak. If one had a problem the others could step in temporarily to take care of what needed to be done. Each of us had a specific job responsibility: management, operations, finance; but each needed to be able to do all three functions. We all learned each aspect of the business and knew every machine, part, worker, supplier, and customer. We each knew bank account balances, and when bills were due. We had to be Jacks-of-All-Trades, because if we weren't, we would likely fail.

And We Did Not Intend To Fail.

The Business Plan included the balance of the factory space gifted to us by our father, for which we had no rent due and the costs we bore were just the maintenance of the facility and the equipment, labor and materials. The older, workable metal fabricating equipment was there for us to use. The key for success was to make a very limited line of shelving

- manageable, salable, priced right, and easy to make. All we needed were a few dies for the shelving parts. We felt we had a win, win situation, going into this new business.

One critical aspect was commitment. We all agreed that if we faced any future adverse situations we would not quit. We would firmly stand behind each other, by each giving 100% of ourselves to the business. We also promised that when we made enough money, we would give our father an investors' share of the profits at the end of each year. This was fair payback for what he gave us: our start.

As far as actual job responsibilities, it was decided that one brother (the financial whiz) would handle the office administration, another (the engineer) would supervise the factory workers and machinery operations, and the third (the planner) would take charge of the marketing and sales and perhaps sourcing on steel materials in the future. That was last one was me. Each to their strengths.

The good part is that we believed we didn't need outside investors, so we had none. We were aided by the fact that two local steel distributors offered to give us open account, on 60-day payment terms. We agreed to it (happily). Then our banker agreed to make a commitment to give us both short and long-term loans to use for inventory and for working capital, subject only to usual and customary bank loan conditions. (Note that usual and customary bank loan conditions require you to commit everything you have to repayment; this destroys you financially if you have to repay personally. More on that later.)

We agreed, all three of us, to continue the corporation under a name we all agreed to – which happened to be the name our father used before retiring. (Oops. Forgot to mention this was the other thing our father "gifted" to us.) We intended to start factory production within the next 60 days. We were ready to commit ourselves fully, and so we were on our way to start the business venture; and on a positive note.

So, why go into business in the first place? You may be that at the stage of life where you want a change. You want to be in charge and make your own decisions. It could be a mid-life crisis (not the best reason but a common one) and that you find you want to do something different in your life so you want to make a career change. Maybe you were fired or laid-off from your job. At any age you could be unhappy with your current employment, but yet you want to continue to do what you're doing in the same field where you already are somewhat expert and knowledgeable. In all of these cases, you want to be your own boss. The only way to do that is to start your own business. So you do.

So, do you have enough passion to succeed? Remember - the secret is 90% hard work and 10% drive and luck. You are taking a risk that you might lose everything you've ever saved and everything you have, all for the chance to be on your own. The leveraging of finances, knowledge of the subject and working your plan determines your success in business. Failure could be due to financial reasons, changes in the economy or in the marketplace selling against other competitors.

If your plan doesn't work out, you can fail. If you time it wrong and just miss the market, you can fail. If you time it wrong and are too early, you can fail. If you are undercapitalized, you can fail. If you don't have a good plan, you can fail. If you have bad luck or a product failure, you can fail.

And if you don't put in the hard work required, you will fail.

So why start your own business? Well, a job in America is no longer necessarily a job for life. Because of that fact many middle managers decide to become small business entrepreneurs. They get buyouts that fund their ideas, or they are cut loose and must find something that fits their skill set. IF no jobs are out there, sometimes starting a small business is the only option other than joblessness. How and where and what you do in this new business depends on when you start your own business, where you live or want to, whether you are single, married, divorced or widowed, or how you lose your current job.

You have to know where you want to go, otherwise, you'll end up traveling anywhere else, and not where you want to end up. And many times, you don't know you're on the wrong road until it's too late to turn back.

You need strategies in business to survive. Henry Ford had a winning strategy in the car business by automating production and finding a way to sell an automobile for a low price so that the masses could buy it and yet still making a profit on each individual sale. A year later, Alfred Sloan of General Motors successfully modified the product by satisfying consumer needs and desires through providing individual custom colors, styles and models instead of Ford's "Any color you want as long as it's black."

You must decide what your winning strategy will be in business. There are questions you need to answer in order to make a final decision for a career change. And it's all about risk. These questions include the following: Are you really doing something you like? What are the potential earnings you can make in what you will choose to do? Are you confident in your present job? Do you feel you are too old for your position? Do you believe that management will decide you are too old so you face being laid off from your job? Can you make enough money at what you choose to do to not only survive but thrive? And, finally, what are the risks if I change my career and then fail; can I get my old job back or find another one like it at similar pay if I cannot succeed on my own?

No matter what you do in business you are taking a risk. You could lose all the money you invested in a new business venture, and fast. It is a fact that less than twenty percent (20%) of all startups survive to their fifth year. That means that over 80% of startup small businesses fail and go out of business in four years or less. The term for that is "Belly Up" which compares your dead business to a dead animal or fish belly up on the ground or beach. To be one of those 20% means hard work, harder work, still more hard work, enough funds to survive lean times and bad patches, and a bit of luck.

Whenever you invest in a new business, you have the risk that you could lose your entire investment, plus the time you put in on your efforts. It takes a great sales person, one with active knowledge and abilities and the confidence in what has to be done, to succeed in a small business.

And most current entrepreneurs are younger than those even just two decades ago. They are better educated, more visionary, and more motivated to work for themselves. Many are experienced in the field they are entering despite their young ages. These are true visionaries, workaholics, and risk takers. For these new entrepreneurs, a small business startup offers them great opportunities.

- - - -

Opening any small business takes a lot of thought in business planning.

When Andrew started his retail copy center business in Maine, he set up shop in his garage. This wasn't unusual because a large number of small businesses in New England are home- or garage- based. They install separate phone and electric lines, and usually separate heating zones. (This is done so the costs of the business can be identified and later deducted for tax purposes on the business return.) These myriad businesses run from an office or area dedicated solely to that business.

Before opening his business, Andrew needed a business plan to outline and identify his proposed line of business and the products and services he would sell. He also needed to identify and project marketing, management, seed capital, cash-flow, sales channels, required equipment and acquisition of the same, and how the business would both survive and thrive. [*My father helped. Couldn't have done it without him.*]

Without a plan, his small business could easily fail, and almost instantly. Of course, a good plan won't save a bad idea or necessarily make you rich by itself, but you do need a good business plan in order to start a small business on a successful course of action. It all begins and ends with **Mr. PHIL.** The business plan. THE BUSINESS PLAN.

You need a "concept." This entails a product or service that you will sell (unique or not) that is either "needed" or "wanted" by your target consumer. And you need to know who that consumer is. Are they the man or woman on the street, or another business? Is your product or service already available in the marketplace? If you sell it, can you make enough sales to reach economies of scale? Can you mark up the product or service far enough above cost to make a sufficient profit to pay all your total expenses AND your salary?

Probably (definitely) the most important (and most common) reason new small businesses fail is the lack of money. Seed capital, investment capital, start-up funds, whatever you call it, it's still just money at the beginning. Either you don't have enough in the beginning or you don't make enough from sales to cover expenses. It is exceptionally rare for a startup to make a profit in their first year; almost all lose money in the beginning. In fact, it takes almost 18 months, on average, for a new business to turn a profit or reach a point where incremental sales produce more revenue they cost. In other words, sales won't cover the costs in the beginning. That could mean that a new owner would not draw a salary for at least the first six months. Or longer. In fact, most business owners fail because they take out a (usually oversized) salary and pay for a lot of expenses (mostly personal) from the business from almost day one. This is a **guaranteed** way to fail. To be successful, most entrepreneurs must defer their salary for as much as eighteen (18) months. And expenses must be minimal and <u>solely business related</u>. (Just ask the IRS.)

The reality of undercapitalization is that most new business owners must be prepared not to draw a salary until the business is profitable. This means they must have enough personal savings to survive for up to 18 months or until the business can afford to pay them without risking insolvency. (Of course, the reward for this is usually higher salaries for owners once it is successful, coupled with a suddenly valuable asset: the business.) Most businesses are not profitable until more than 12 months have passed.

Most businesses have a storefront - a physical location which they own or rent (rent is more easily deducted) - to do business. It is relatively easy (but not necessarily cheap) to set up shop in your garage. Andrew spent tens of thousands on construction, upgrades, and equipment before the copy center even opened. A small business flower shop in a home garage near Andrew's location had two coolers and a cash register to conduct their business, along with a separate phone, power and Internet line. (The copy center had 24 machines plus computers and business supplies, and, of course, that all important cash register.)

To open a business, you also need government approval and licenses. This is usually the second most difficult part after the capital. You must incorporate (unless you are a fool who wishes to be sued personally; see Chapter 5) and you must register with each state where you will do business. You incorporate in your "home" state, but may have to do the same in other states if you want the rights granted to registered businesses that include the right to sue clients or customers who don't pay you, or if you need to collect and remit sales tax. You also need to have incorporation documents, and almost always revenue and tax licenses from each aforementioned state. You will also need a Tax Identification Number ("T.I.N.") from the IRS (this is a sort of Social Security Number for businesses). You may also need municipal government's business/ property licenses and occupancy permits, permits for signage and construction, and if your business concerns food or food service or any form of fluids, health and environmental permits and certifications. These are rarely from the same office and usually involve dozens of separate forms and filings - and fees. And if you don't file on time or file taxes or tax payments on time, you can be fined, put out of business, or even jailed by the respective governments.

This is why I again repeat the necessity to have expert advisers such as an accountant and an attorney available and able to assist you in both the establishment, and ongoing operation, of your new business.

You will then have to meet the "marketplace" which is to say you will have to seek customers and face competition. Oftentimes, to meet change in the marketplace, you will have to change with it, to be at the cutting edge of the changing economy. You have to set your goals and your objectives to get there. You may have to modify your strategies due to changing markets or products or services in your plan.

Remember - there are no safety nets on any businesses - and that applies equally to both every business already out there, and to the business you own, start, and run yourself. And being an Entrepreneur involves good financial planning, being informed on the products or services you sell and what flows in and out, to achieve your profits and your goals; one of which is cash-flow. You will need money to pay your bills, to pay your employees and yourself. Cash-flow management is critical, and money is at the root of the whole equation.

- - - -

The 10 Point Business Plan

Below is an outline version of a 10-Point Business Plan.

The BUSINESS PLAN consists of

1. Executive Summary
2. Company Description
3. Market Analysis
4. Product and Services
5. Marketing and Sales

6. Operations
7. Management and Ownership
8. Organization and Personnel
9. Funds Required and Uses
10. Financial Data

Here is the template to follow to make a business plan, a written document to clearly define the goals of the business. The 10 outlined categories, the methods of achieving it and describes what the business does, how it will be done, who has to do it, where it will be done, why it's being done and where it will be completed.

1   EXECUTIVE SUMMARY. Outline the important parts of your plan to attract financial funders, its purpose, 2 or 3 pages at the most, avoid fancy words, wild claims, unnecessary charts to take away from creditability and no slick plans.

2   COMPANY DESCRIPTION. What type of business is it, merchandising, manufacturing or service? Status of the business: start up, expansion or takeover. Form the business takes: Sole proprietor, partnership or corporation. Why will your business be profitable?

3   MARKET ANALYSIS. Product definition, trade area, market sales volume, trade area customers, competition, key to successful location(s), price and quality

4   PRODUCTS and SERVICE. Describe your products or services, state value to the user of your products or services, compare competing products or services, summarize the costs of your products and   describe intellectual property.

5   MARKETING and SALES. Target Market geographic/industry/type of buyer, pricing strategies and distribution.

6   OPERATIONS. How company produces products or services. Required physical facility (location/expansion potential, lease or purchase machinery needed, requirements needed for layout and floor plan, costs to install, renovate utility costs and security costs.

7   MANAGEMENT and OWNSHIP. Resources to management: Advisors, consultants, networking, mastermind group (2 or more people), accountant, banker. Look for business background, experience, personal   and financial data.

8   ORGANIZATION and PERSONNEL. Carefully select your staff and reward them well; travel/treat them as individuals worthy of respect.

9   FUNDS REQUIRED and USE. How will the loan be spent i.e. working capital, new equipment, inventory or supplies, etc. Who are the suppliers and do you get 3 quotes on each purchase?

10   FINANCIAL DATA. Breakout the Proforma balance sheet/sales/profit and loss and cash-flow. Get an idea of industry ratio from your accountant.

- - - -

My brother was right – "MOST PEOPLE DO NOT PLAN TO FAIL; THEY FAIL TO PLAN."

You must try to create and develop a strong Business Plan from the 10 Point Business Plan above, by researching the field of the business you will be going into, its sales and marketing of those products or services and the finances you will need.

Be prepared ahead of time to sell your plan. Write your business plan up at least several weeks before you present it to your financial sources, whether to a banker or to an outside private lending source.

Know as you grow, about the proposal you intend to sell or the service you will be offering. Your estimated CASH-FLOW is an important key to show your lender you can pay back the loan, in a specific period of time. Remember, a good business plan provides a benchmark for a financial lender to inspect and approve or disapprove your loan.

You should also gain knowledge in the following key areas:

A. Advertising and marketing

B. Bookkeeping

C. Time Management

D. Purchasing

E. Employee training

F. Customer relations training

If you need help on these concerns or with the Business Plan in general, you can get professional assistance from your CPA accountant, lawyer, friendly non-business or business associate, colleges, even the US Small Business Administration or your local municipal government; all can provide ideas and counseling. It is also suggested you join industry-related trade groups and attend trade shows, industrial meetings or workshops, in the field you intend to enter.

- - - -

In the next Chapter (5) we will discuss the actual basics of launching your new business.

CHAPTER FIVE
Launching Your Own New Business

George Bernard Shaw once said "There are two sources of happiness in life. One is not getting what you want; the other is getting it." As startup small businesses, you will experience both.

It was always my philosophy to make lots of money and own lots of businesses, while helping others make it, too. As a joke, I said "I'd like to go into the business of scissors grinding, because that business thrives when things are dull." (A good real-life example? The real estate business.)

People don't grow old merely by living a number of years. People also grow old by deserting their ideals. Years wrinkle the skin, but to give up one's entrepreneurial enthusiasm wrinkles the soul. No matter what your age, there is in every human being's heart that love to obtain new ideas. It is the sweetest amazement to think of the challenges that lie ahead in the game of life.

As entrepreneurs, all of us have much in common. We are the risk takers. We should be the hardest workers; the "do-it-all people." We're the spirit of the great American dream, being in our own small business. We owe that obligation to instill the spirit and drive in each future entrepreneur's desire for fame, fortune and success in ourselves and in others.

Starting new small businesses are very challenging. When we have an idea to do something, full or part-time, we should intend to make it a full-time venture. Here are three ways an Entrepreneur can go into business. You can do any or all three of them: (1) Start-up your own business; (2) Buy an existing business; and/or (3) Establish a franchise relationship (which can also fall under (1) above).

Starting up Your Own Business

In life, you need to reflect on where you have been and where you would like to go in the future. Perhaps you need "a wake-up call" to maximize that thinking in order to start a part- or full- time business of your own. Some years ago, when I was lecturing at Philadelphia's Temple University Business School on "How to Start Your Own Business," it was amazing to see the age spread of the attendees, from as young as 18 to as old as 67 years of age. These men and women were interested not only in going into retailing but wholesaling, manufacturing, service and consulting businesses, as well as varied home-based small businesses. A good and varied mix, to be sure. They all were "waking up" to the prospect of running their own business.

Starting your own business is an exciting decision for those who want not just to be employed, but to be their own boss. Oftentimes money is not the driving factor in the choice to start your own business but rather the goal is to be in control of your own destiny. Money is a great validation of your ability and also is wonderful to use to pay your bills, but is not always the driving motivation. Sometimes it comes down to what one enjoys, and enjoys doing with a passion to be successful. Sometimes it's just being able to do something different or using an idea no one else is willing to pursue. But all of these have something in common for the successful entrepreneur: business involves an understanding of the skills applicable to that specific business operation. Most successful entrepreneurs have prior work experience in the field they enter, yet some do not.

Here are three examples of people who started their own businesses without any prior experience in those fields. It should help to show why experience is always preferable to a "cold" start, but how it can be overcome by hard work (and even harder work).

The first was a couple, a husband and wife who happened to attend my lecture together. They wanted to open a linen and box goods store. After a year and a half, it was a thriving business and became a real moneymaker for them. They had started a niche business that was both fun, and profitable. And they made it by merchandising the old fashion way - phone calling, literature drops at local churches, small ads in the classified newspaper sections, word of mouth, soliciting all the local caterers for potential leads. The secret was a practical, gorilla-marketing program. And they worked. Hard.

The second was a middle-aged man who clerked at a computer store chain. He left that job to enter a business that distributed electrically lighted signs to commercial businesses. His father-in-law had died, leaving no one to run the one-person business. The man learned some important principles of operating a small business from things I taught at my lecture. Afterward, a consultant he met at the lecture gave him free advice when he needed it during his first year doing the work. That business grew successfully, eventually employing 12 additional workers. His secret for success was a good business plan and a base of loyal customers on which to build. And, of course, hard work.

The third example was an attendee who was married to a singer/actress. He wanted to give his wife a "boost" by producing her first record album. He used the principles learned at the lecture to assist him in finding the information he needed to give him the knowledge on how to market and finance their record album enterprise. The basic secret in their business was to get money to adequately finance the venture, and to make contacts in the industry who would actually give them a chance. This, of course, was accomplished by both finding the money and by doing the hard work involved to make it happen!

Don't be misled by these success stories, however. As I said before: less than 20% of small businesses are still around after five years; all of the rest fail. It is a tough world for the unprepared. To make it, you have to work hard, put in long hours, work hard, follow a solid and well-prepared business plan, work hard, be focused, learn about the business - and the field, work hard, make sure you are adequately capitalized, work hard, be just a bit lucky, and work hard. (Notice a trend?)

Any deviation from this is likely to result in your new business being one of those 4 out of 5 that fail.

Anyone not prepared to work not twice but three times as hard as the hardest-working employee is destined for failure. New business owners must be prepared to be (and must in fact be) the first one in in the morning, the last one out in the evening, a master of everything about the business, and the one who not only must, but WILL, make the hard decisions. The buck, as they say, stops with you. And you must be willing to take personal responsibility for every decision both good and bad. You must also be ready to suffer for mistakes (and be prepared to have some) no new business will be perfect and smooth, and anyone who says you will not have problems that demand hard choices is lying to you. Hiring, firing, cuts and expansion all have some pain attached.

An entrepreneurial spirit is kindled for everyone with a dream, to start a business for themselves. For people already in business who want to sharpen their business skills and improve their savvy and business performance? This is accomplished by learning the latest cutting-edge techniques, refining and honing your strategic business planning, identifying new customers, improving advertising and marketing promotions, coming up with new pricing ideas, and, of course, finding new and inventive ways to maintain or get new business financing sources.

Sometimes you do something different to be successful, like by being outside the cookie jar, as Debbie Fields, founder of Mrs. Fields Cookies, who had outlets in most shopping malls and airports around the country, did.

I had a conversation with her back in the 1990's. I frequently ask people why they do what they do. [*Andrew does the same thing…*] So, I asked Mrs. Fields "How did you start your business?" Her reply still amazes me. She told me the first two days she opened her store, no one came in to buy any cookies. No one! It looked like she would be out of business before she ever got started. So what did she do?

Near the end of the second day, she went outside and gave away all her cookies, at no charge, to people walking by her store. What a simple marketing solution. Free samples. But that one idea was the start of an extraordinary retail empire.

Whether on purpose or out of desperation, her marketing tactic has stayed with me all my business life. I realized that (all pun intended) the "one-size-fits-all cookie-cutter" approach doesn't fit everyone and doesn't provide all businesses with a perfect solution. Whether the cookies would go stale after the first day or the idea of letting people try the sample cookies while they were fresh does not matter.

Debbie (Mrs.) Fields broke the biggest marketing roadblock, getting people to try her products. It was the basics of marketing that formed her success in retailing. Her products are still sold today, and are very profitable. All from a little spark to not let cookies go to waste and instead of being stubborn and waiting for business to come to her, she went to them and gave away her wastable products before they wasted. And she traded her samples for a viable and "tasty" victory in the business world.

The "whatever it takes" attitude shown by Mrs. Fields is what a new business has to do to be successful. In her case, getting people to taste the cookies was what mattered most. Any product that is sold to a consumer must be marketed by its look and feel to insure repeat sales. The best way is by getting it into the hands of the consumer by any means necessary, even free. As shown by her success, it worked.

Sometimes you need to give a sample of your product, or service, to the consumer, to be accepted in the marketplace. Perhaps a special offer or special terms. Any special service makes the customer feel a "personal connection" so they will want the product will help you to build repeat orders. But the most important selling feature is just to get out there, hustle, and work hard. Find ways to locate and keep customers. Keep them with high customer service standards, quality products, and responsiveness to customer wants.

Put yourself in the mindset of your customer: what does your customer like, or dislike? Whether a certain type of cookie (like Mrs. Fields) or a specific product or service, loyalty is the key word in marketing. Loyal customers come back. Irritated ones do not. And, it is harder to get a new customer than keep a current one. And much costlier.

Whether you work in a full-time business or a part-time hobby, and whether for mega-profits or just a bit of extra income, employing marketing basics lets you stand head and shoulders above the crowd. You need to think, live, and do a "can do" attitude - at all times.

The real answer in marketing is to establish a goal to reach, and then reach for it. Make a business plan that you can follow like a road map. Make it readable and sufficiently detailed enough to provide what you need to succeed, and then follow it. Be committed 100% in spirit and in work ethic to be successful. It takes long hours, hard work and perseverance on your part. Or as the saying goes "(A)nything worth doing, is worth doing well." Oh so true!

A lot of fundamentals in marketing are transferable, in networking through business and trade group meetings, golf outings or business expos, you can benefit by sharing strategies with others. Know your product strengths and weaknesses against competition-quality wise, price-wise and delivery-wise. Gauge your market share. Things happen fast with competition. When you have a real winner, others quickly copy your product or service. Be prepared to move quickly in the marketplace. Sometimes you even need to adjust your prices (and profit margins) up or down to meet slow volume or high margin sales; all to meet your customer's needs, as well as to keep them as customers.

Think of Mrs. Fields the next time you have a problem. Get outside of the cookie jar, and meet your customer. It really pays off.

In this world, there is nothing constant but change. That goes for online marketing like buying ads on Facebook, Twitter, Google, and other tech platforms. Changes constantly occur in ways to improve inventory management, employee recruitments and retention, computing and other technology, financial analysis, and even products and services. Be prepared for these changes. And be proactive.

The "Home" Front as your Edge

For those of you who are thinking to start your own business, either out of necessity, being laid off from your present job, recently retired, or just burned out, think about working from home. When you get the itch to keep active or need the extra income, take the plunge into working at home. It costs less, and it can give you a quick start.

My friend was laid off after 20 years of being employed by the same company. Due to economic conditions, the company downsized and eliminated his office position. The saving grace was his wife's income from a fulltime job with a local insurance agency. He knew how to talk to customers because of his experience as a customer service manager at his former company. So after he was let go, he decided to set up an office in his home to do what he did best - while investing a lot less money to do so.

There are many things to cover in setting up an office out of a home. Several daily important concerns have to be addressed, whether you are a sales person, representing a service or product or part-time small business entrepreneur. The biggest issue to consider is whether or not you will set up an office in your home and whether or not you will make it bona fide so that you can expense the costs of that office on your tax return. You will have to organize your time and determine if you will be happy doing business from your home. And you will have to make sure you pass the IRS's significant Home Office tax deductibility test to ensure you don't run afoul of the IRS and be penalized.

There are lots of benefits to working from home. No travel time, low overhead (no rent), reduced or no heat and electric to pay as you would for outside office space. Phone and Internet are covered, too. Or are they? Tax wise, business expenses can be deducted: supplies, insurance, utilities, phone, Internet, and office space used in your home are all deductible provided you can prove that all (including the space you use for the home office) were used SOLELY for business: and a business whose intent was to generate taxable income. All these deductions are subject to the keeping of adequate records for IRS purposes. Of course, you will need proper space in which to work, in an uninterrupted atmosphere. And proof of separation of the office expenses from personal ones. (This really is a trap and a serious audit red-flag. The IRS typically audits a much higher percentage, i.e. most, of home office deduction returns.) On the investment side, you need a phone(s), desk(s) and chairs, a computer and printer, office supplies, filing cabinet and office copier.

However, assume for a minute that taxes are not an issue and you will be using a home office in any event. So how do you organize your time working at home? You will need to plan a work schedule, to start at a specific time each day and stick to it. Plan your day in advance. Dress as if you were going out to a regular office, not in pajamas. Map out your time and STICK TO YOUR SCHEDULE. The biggest problem faced by home office workers is that they are cavalier about it and don't take it seriously because "I'm at home" and with the myriad distractions and lackadaisical attitude they are destined to fail. So, to prevent this, dress up as if you were meeting a client. Have a door to your office, and close it when working so you do not have distractions. Leave the office to get lunch. DO NOT EAT AT YOUR DESK! And keep kids and pets out when working.

Next is how to take your being at this "isolated" location and turn that into an advantage. To solve day-to-day problems, network with others that operate noncompetitive but similar type home businesses. Talk to a former colleague or friend you trust, to feedback ideas on what to do in perplexing matters. Networking is critical. This can be done by using a business networking organization that is local or national, from a local business lunch group to the Toastmasters or the Rotary or regular meetings set up by the local Better Business Bureau ("BBB"). And join that BBB for two reasons: to show community connection ("I'm a member of the local BBB") and for the benefits they provide small businesses like meet-and-greets, group insurance and banking plans, and other benefits. Being a BBB member means that you have been "vetted" (or at least customers will think so" and that you adhere to a high standard of business ethics that will make customers more inclined to trust you, and to use your business.

Set a goal to talk to a specific number of prospects and customers each day. Make phone calls and not just e-mails. Do it on a routine basis. This means daily. And whenever you can, get out of your office to network with people (like in local charitable, social, or networking organizations to meet new people). Plan this just like any other item on your schedule. I would recommend you join at least three organizations (always try to make one a non-profit or charity) and attend meetings at least twice per month in each (unless they meet less often).

Make sure you are lean and mean, but despite that make sure you spend the money on a top-tier computer with more memory and storage than you ever think you will need and on Internet and phone plans that are business-level. (Many cable companies have double or triple play programs which make subscribing to them both cheaper than individual subscriptions and provide faster or more optioned service.) Spend liberally on your office desk and chair since you will spend at least a third of your life sitting there. Get a first-rate phone with a speaker and an answering system. And make sure you keep receipts for these and all your office supplies, and be certain that you don't mix business services and items with personal ones.

AND KEEP IT ALL BUSINESS WHEN IN YOUR HOME OFFICE. NO EXCEPTIONS!!!!!

So now you are ready to start your home-based business, with no employees to worry about at the beginning but you, until the business grows. (Remember not to pay yourself an initial salary unless you have enough revenue right at the beginning. Only salary yourself once you have enough revenue.)

For those who are retired or unemployed at the moment, the time to start is NOW. You can fund it using your savings, credit card, or find other ways to initially finance your new small business, but it must be funded. And you must have enough to live on until after the start-up have sufficient revenue to pay your salary and payroll taxes. Maybe you can get a partner who will invest with you. Or for a really low-cost entry, start the business by e-mail from your home. You can do that even while keeping your present job by starting it as a part-time venture. Many small businesses start out as hobbies that expand when the owner finds that it can be expanded into a full-time job.

Rudyard Kipling once wrote "they tried to copy my mind, but I always left them six months behind." Got a small business idea that is right for you that will cost just a few thousand dollars to start? If you can afford it, then start it right away. Remember that starting your own business means no dollars paid for goodwill; the business is created in your own image. You should have the ability to finance it, since ever thing is new. The value is what you invest plus your own hard work.

Below is a list of potential small businesses you can start in the personal services, retail, tech, and hobby fields that can initially be run from your home using just a desk, car, computer, phone; and little money. (Note: some of these vocations require licensing or advanced certification.)

Accounting Services
Appliance Technician
Arts and Crafts
Attorney Services
Auto Graveyard
Babysitting/Childcare Service
Baseball Cards
Bookkeeping
Carpenter or Handyman Lawn
Maintenance
Catering Services
Computer Repair
Consultant (in any field)
Cosmetics (Make or Sell)
Electrical Services
Gift Wrapping

Graphic Design
Healthcare Services
Home Cleaning Service
Home Remodeling
Host a Flea/Farmers' Market
House or Room Rental
Interior Design
Jewelry Making
Maintenance Services
Pet Care/Pet Sitting / Walking
Website Design/Management
Shoe Repair
Sidewalk Food/Farm Stand
Software Developer
Stamps, Coins, and Bills
Used Furniture Sales

STRATEGIES FOR STARTUPS OR CONTINUING SMALL BUSINESSES

Typically, you will need some preparation before you rush headlong into your new vocation. The following are things you will need to obtain or attain prior to starting or acquiring your new business, and you should begin to acquire the knowledge or assets or connections NOW for the following:

Get experience in the field you want to enter. The best way get experience is to go to work for someone else already in that business. It takes the average person about one year to learn any business, and two years to become proficient in it to the point you could run it or start one of your own. You might need more or less time depending on how quickly and how well you learn and pick up the necessary skills, but these times are the average. There is no replacement for experience.

Line up sources of supply. Without them you can't stay in business. You need to know who to buy from, how to buy from them, what they require to sell to you, what terms are customary in your chosen industry, what the costs are for the product and for delivery (if applicable) and what financial proofs your supplier will require both before – and after - they start selling to you. Personal contacts are critical for this factor, and getting to know a few suppliers or their representatives personally is irreplaceable.

Line up working capital. Don't start unless you have money for at least six month's overhead and four month's inventory. And then try to acquire more than that in upfront funds, if possible. These amounts are an absolute and unalterable minimum. A year's worth of advance funding for both overhead and inventory is better. 18 months is preferable if you can find it, but frequently that much is unobtainable. And do not expect to take a salary for up to 18 months (until you are profitable); have enough personal savings to cover that. That first six months you will almost certainly lose money. The first year is generally the minimum breakeven time for almost all new startups. Financial ratios and turnover of inventory (all of which also need to be identified and discussed in your Business Plan) will provide costs of goods (divided by) average inventory; inventory (divided by) net working capital will give you the R.O.I. (Return on Investment). You need to know these numbers, and these terms. Once you have calculated them, you can check your numbers against competitor profiles issued by Dun & Bradstreet, stock brokerages like Schwab, or other rating firms.

Build credit sources. Now. Before you go into business, set up charge accounts in department stores. Open a small checking account. Get gas credit cards. Try NOT to pay cash on the spot, for whatever you buy. Pay with credit, pay your bills on time, and you will get known for being an "on-time payer" of money you owe. Paying your bills on time develops credit which is critical to your being able to borrow money or get lenders or investors to provide you the necessary financial resources to succeed. Do the same for your new business by setting up business accounts and paying them on time too.

If you currently rent a house or apartment, try (if you can afford) to buy a house to establish both a firm location and creditworthiness. If you are single and find the right person, get married. No kidding! You are a better loan risk in the eyes of a banker. Having a permanent address is a benefit to both your credit report and in the eyes of lenders and employers. Owning a property means that there will be at least some equity you can use to collateralize against a loan for your business.

Get a partner if you can to diversify your risk and double your chances. If you are experienced in the proposed business but lack money, get a partner with money (a silent or working partner). If you're not experienced but have money, get a working partner who knows the business, even if he or she doesn't have much money but is knowledgeable or experienced in your industry. They should invest at least a token amount to guarantee they will perform; this is known as having "skin in the game" meaning they'll be more likely to work hard (and succeed) if they have something to lose just as you do. The more they have invested the more they have to lose and the more dedicated they'll be in spending the time and effort to make the business succeed.

Deal with suppliers who give you terms. "Dating on a floor plan" or "field warehousing" are ways in which you take things on consignment or otherwise can stall payments until at least some of the goods have sold. You are working off the supplier's credit extension and this is better than a bank because there is usually no additional cost (like interest or fees) to do this. Retailers do this all the time, routinely getting 30 to 90 days to pay for delivered goods, but sometimes even more time. This course of action is smart, especially if you have not yet built up a credit background. You are allowing a supplier to use you as a warehouse and getting goods on "credit" for your effort. See if you can buy cooperatively by joining a buying group or a trade group that will help you get information on market conditions, sources, etc., and also buy in higher quantities for the entire group thus getting you better prices and terms than you could do on your own. Wakefern Corporation (the cooperative buying group for Shoprite supermarkets) is one example of a buying cooperative. Shoprite is not a franchise or a corporation but rather a bunch of individual store owners who work together through a "mutual" type buying cooperative to provide all stores with the same acquisitional pricing and terms whether a member owns one or twenty stores. This serves to lower costs because you buy in bulk, thereby getting bulk discounts.

Location! Location! Location! Finding the right location is one of the most important aspects of your new business, and is nearly everything if it is a retail establishment dependent on customers coming to you to buy. (Think of fast food restaurants.) Check your intended location for traffic patterns that affect your business. This is especially important for a retail store or restaurant. Prime locations = increased business.

Try to buy an established business rather than starting a new one up cold. Most new businesses operate "in the red" in their first year. This means they lose money. This comes from the red ink used by accountants to denote losses and the black ink used to denote profits. To be "in the black" you must be making an operating profit, which is a profit on each incremental sale. This is critical: if you cannot fund operating in the red then you must acquire a business which makes a profit from the first day you acquire it. Remember that almost all new businesses lose money in their first year, and so will yours.

And lastly, work like hell. You can make it a successful business, if you follow your business plan, work your tail off, and get some good fortune.

Buying an existing Small Business

You can go into business two ways: you can start a business (or franchise) or you can buy an existing one. Most existing businesses that are sold are sold for one of three reasons: 1) the founder or owner wants to retire (or has died) and there is no one working in the business or close to the owner who can (or is willing to) take over, 2) the company is losing money and needs a new owner with cash to try to make the business succeed before it goes bankrupt, or 3) someone offers the current owner so much money (sometimes more than it is really worth) that they cash out and sell and take the money. Most small businesses fall in the first category, a small percentage in the second category, and almost none in the last category.

Buying an existing business gives you some advantages over starting up one from scratch, or "greenfielding" a business. It means that there is a track record, and that you can see their past years' performance. Their employees are experienced and know how to operate the business. The services or products are clear, defined, and proven. What you are buying is clearly delineated and visible. Customers and suppliers are not just known, but as familiar with the business as the business is with them. And the real estate or lease is already there and in place so no location issues distract from operations. In short, buying a going concern is easier because all of the pieces of the puzzle are already there and in their proper place. But that does not mean it is always smooth.

While you could pick up a bargain, depending on why the business is being offered for sale (due to retirement, shortage of funds or a change by the present owner to sell or retire or otherwise want or need money themselves), the fact is that most small businesses are as much an extension of the personality of the seller as they are an independent operation. The personalities always matter and the personal interactions between owner, supplier, and customer matter deeply. Sometimes this requires a new owner to receive a transition period after the purchase where the seller will stay on for a few months to a year and "introduce" the new owner to the suppliers and key customers so they feel comfortable and at ease with the new owner. Sometimes this is not possible, such as when an owner dies and the business has to be sold for tax or estate purposes or because no heirs know how to work in or run the business, or know nothing about it at all other than that they just inherited something of value that can be sold. Here, the risks are almost the same as a new business in that some things are out of the buyer's control and there is a real risk that it won't work out and the business could still fail.

To determine the matters to be addressed in the purchase of an existing business, there are important things a potential buyer or new investor needs to know. They must research a lot, but specifically the following important subjects: Track record, staff, products, seller financing, and if the real estate is free of debt or if the buyer must assume a mortgage, lease, or other liabilities of the seller.

- - - -

Harry's real-life story is of a businessman who bought an existing small business that he grew into a big business. When he eventually sold it, he was incredibly wealthy. Harry had a philosophy: "Work is love made visible." And work he did, both from home and on the job.

My wife and I met with Harry many times. One of the things I liked best about him was that he was not a spendthrift, but that he was frugal. [*The difference between frugal and cheap is that someone frugal looks for a good bargain but will choose quality over price where possible, whereas someone who is cheap will always choose price over everything. I am often frugal, Scrooge is cheap.*] He could afford anything he wanted, but he watched his pennies and ran his business in much the same way.

On one occasion we invited him to have dinner with us at an upscale restaurant. "Oh no" he said. "That's too expensive." Instead, he asked us to come to his home and join him for his specialty of the house, a simple homemade casserole. It was the best casserole we had ever eaten. And cheaper.

Harry played sports in high school. A quarterback, he learned how to be a leader. It paid off handsomely later in life. "Winning is all about teamwork. I learned that in high school and it's worked for me my entire life." His philosophies carried into his later years when he owned businesses, and he was successful in all of them. Teamwork was Harry's buzzword. He grew his businesses because he believed in teamwork. Employees, managers, and partners all worked with him, not for him. And all prospered. He put his faith in the people he worked with and it paid off for him and for his companies. When he died his estate was worth a fortune, and true to his beliefs, he shared much of it with his workers, his family, and his beloved charities. I should be so lucky. (A long, long time from now on that last part.)

We once persuaded Harry to bring his family to that expensive restaurant and join us for dinner. He again demurred, but after some gentle prodding by me and my wife, he came and ate and smiled the whole time. His eldest quietly told me on the side "I'm really glad you got my father to come here for dinner. He's turned it down time and again because he always said it was too expensive. Thanks for finally getting him to try it at least once." He was a small-town boy made good, and knew many famous people who he called by their first name while at the same time they always called him "Mr."

Harry was one heck of a great guy, both in business and in his community. He taught me a lot. He was humble, honorable, and successful. He was my friend. And I miss him.

Establishing a FRANCHISE Business

So, you are finally ready to get into your own business, but you want something that you can "hit the ground running" with. That's where the venerable "Franchise" comes in.

A franchise is a business that is mostly "turnkey" (literally, you put the key in and turn it and the door opens and the business runs). Someone else has figured out all the hows and whys and wheres and put them into a business plan that only lacks your name and your location. You pay money to the franchisor (the person or company that set this up and provides the plan, and sometimes the equipment, land, and supplies) and they set you up in business or assist you in doing so. And these myriad franchisors must have a lot of experience in doing so. According to the statistia.com website, there were an estimated 759,236 "franchise establishments" in the United States in 2018. This number has been rising for the last five years after dropping from a high of roughly 774,000 in 2008 to just under 698,000 in 2013.

The franchisor gives the new small business investor the edge to succeed by preparing a plan for how to start a business in a specific trade. The most well-known of these are fast food chains like McDonald's, Wendy's or Burger King. They also include a wide and varied choice of businesses in almost any trade or service. From restaurants to dry cleaners to movers to house cleaners there are literally thousands of franchise ideas to choose from. Franchisors engineer a complete product or service line, so you don't have to. They have management expertise from having done it so that when you buy your franchise, you can hit the ground running. They supply technical help, updates, management and initial employee training, sales and profit projections, and production and operational guidance. Many also provide advertising and sales promotions or help the new franchisee to do so. And a number of them sell the raw materials for the products that are sold or the services that are provided. In fact, since uniformity is key to franchise success, many franchisors either require the franchisees to buy many supplies directly from them, or from a specific set of authorized providers.

So how do franchisors make money? Not just from the franchise fee. Franchisors also require franchisees to pay a royalty from sales to the franchisor. The amount varies but is usually between 4-10 percent of total (gross) revenue, although some charge more or less. For example, Wendy's royalty is 4% of gross revenue, plus another 4% toward advertising. This is paid by franchisees weekly, monthly, or quarterly, depending on the franchise agreement. While usually paid from gross revenue whether or not there is a profit, some allow payments from net revenue, but at a much higher percentage.

This is of course in addition to the initial franchise fee and the initial costs to start the business. And most franchisors require at least some of the funds used to start the business (and pay the initial franchise fee) be your own money and not borrowed. They require elaborate and highly detailed disclosures of your assets, investible cash, work history, and want to know where you are getting your initial funds from and under what terms. And top franchises require you to put a substantial percentage of your own money into it. McDonald's, for example, requires that at least 40% of the initial cost of from $700,000 - $1,500,000 to be your own money that you can prove you did not borrow. This makes you share in the substantial risk of loss so you have a high incentive to do the work necessary to make it be successful. And all of that is on top of the 4% of gross revenue royalty plus at least another 4% (or more) for advertising support. And there are the fees. There are thousands of dollars of annual fees for things like software, compliances, certificates, approvals, and support fees. And these are just to McDonald's. And that does not even include the property rent.

Franchisors can also raise their royalties and fees. They also usually have a limit on time; most franchise agreements only allow you to operate for

15-20 years, and then the franchisor has a right to cancel your franchise rights and close your business, take it over and force it to be sold, or grant you a shorter-term renewal. This renewal, of course, sometimes comes with a new franchise fee. (They're not stupid.) And this is all in addition to any governmental fees and permit charges, professional fees, taxes, and all of the other costs you will incur.

And franchisors do want you to be successful, despite all of this apparent one-sidedness, but for very selfish reasons. If one franchisee goes under quickly or gets a bad reputation it harms everyone - the entire company as well as every other franchisee. Reputation and uniformity are the two most important things that come with a franchise, so there is a huge incentive for the franchisor to make sure when you buy your franchise that you won't destroy their reputation or damage other franchisees and effectively kill the other gooses that are laying those golden eggs that the franchisor can cash in. So, for franchisors, there is a huge incentive to vet out (weed out) problems and likely failures early in the franchisee-purchase process, and prevent their marquee and reputation from being damaged or destroyed by one bad actor or catastrophic failure. And since the government requires franchisors to provide proformas by way of Prospectus to each and every potential franchisee, they want that Prospectus to show only successes, even though they will claim (because they have to) that not everyone will succeed or even do as well as the average for other franchises. "Some may fail."

Make sure it isn't you.

So, you have decided to buy a franchise. How do you choose the one to invest in? How do you value it, either as an initial franchise or by buying one that is already running (which almost always requires the franchisor to sign off and collect a transfer fee)? And, HOW WILL YOU PAY FOR IT?

Choose wisely. A good choice for a franchise is one that you worked in, patronize regularly, or like the concept of. Remember that you will spend half of the rest of your working life there. Prior work experience in a franchise gives you insight into how it is run and what the problems might be ahead of time. A franchise you patronize regularly is one where you can see who buys their products or services and where you have some customer-side knowledge of the likelihood of repeat or continuing business. If you like the concept, you will be more inclined to want to work there and push the franchise and the benefits of the business to potential and regular customers.

Next is the question of valuation. Methods that I used in the past to value businesses we purchased included Market Cost, Cost to Create, Sum of Assets, Goodwill, and Cash-flow Multiples.

Any valuation is dependent on two things, past performance and future likely performance. The latter is more important but only the first, past performance, is positively attainable. Gross sales, net profits, cash-flow, and public valuations of competing similar businesses are the best ways to predict current value. But you must also have some idea of what the future will hold both short- and long-term. If you cannot predict with some reasonably certainty that the business will remain stable or grow then it has little value above liquidation.

For most franchise businesses, the franchisee usually puts in between 25% to 50% of the initial funding in cash from their own savings or assets, with the balance being bank financed through personal or business loans. The franchisee's personal contribution amount may vary depending on the products or services involved and the contract terms of the franchise agreement.

Franchise owners also need their own business plan (separate from the one in the Prospectus). They need strategy, marketing, projected sales, and other details normally found in a business plan. Don't expect the franchisor to provide one and even if they do you still need to have YOUR OWN PLAN!

There are of course costs to running this venture as there are for any business. There is overhead to be covered, rent and salaries to be paid, phone and Internet charges, accountant and attorney and other professional fees, insurance, advertising and marketing costs, and permit and operating fees. These are just some of the costs that should be accounted for in your Plan.

How will you measure gross and net income? What will your pricing be and do you have the freedom to vary it to the market? Will you be taking depreciation allowances on any machinery or property? What about interest payments on your loan and payments of royalty and other fees? Can they be paid from revenue or will there not be enough? Remember that the rule about covering your own salary still applies: be prepared not to take one for up to a year or more until the business is prospering.

Finally, remember that each franchise – and each franchise agreement – is different. The details, costs, and requirements depend on your products or services, and the requirements of the franchisor.

Basic Legal Corporate Structures for Your Business

Startup small and large businesses use any one of these seven business structures (six of which are legal in nature) for many reasons that can include how they are taxed, what legal protections they give to ownership, how easy or difficult they are to manage, who manages, and which state they are formed in. Note that some states do not allow all of these corporate forms; a few do not require a "qualifier" such as "Inc." or "Co." after the name. In my own businesses, we used more than one of these corporate forms depending on when, where, why, and how they were formed, and sometimes tax ramifications.

Also, you need to think of a name. Names are registered at the state level, not nationally. Each state has rules, and you must register in each state where you intend to do business so you are protected, and can get tax and revenue accounts to pay sales and income taxes to those states. (Yes, you will pay income taxes, and collect and remit sales taxes, to each and every state in which you do business if they have such taxes.) And what about your name? Can you just open as "Acme Widgets?" No. Each business in that state must have a unique name. For example, a local McDonald's restaurant may actually be incorporated as "My Mother's Inheritance Was Invested Here By George d.b.a. ("doing business as" and also known as a "Trade Name") McDonalds of 32nd Street." Or "Acme Plumbing of Stanley Avenue." The d.b.a. can be a registered fictitious name, such as "Copy Me" or Plumber's Experts" or Food Rite or any other name which appears on a sign, business cards, and advertising. This allows the business to use a shorter or more publicly acceptable (or less confusing) name, while receiving checks or other payments, as well as promotional opportunities, under the trade name. All this is provided for when you create and register a business with your state, usually through the Secretary of State's office or the Revenue Department of the state. Some states do not allow d.b.a.'s, and some, like

Maine, do not require the "qualifier" of Inc. or Co. or Company that most states do require. In Maine, Mercy Me I'm a Company, Inc. doesn't need the "Inc." behind it, but most elsewhere you do. Once you clear your chosen name and d.b.a. (sometimes referred to as a "fictitious name") with the Secretary of State's office or the Bureau of Corporations (usually it's one of the two) you are ready to incorporate. Now all you have to do is figure out which type of form is best for your situation. (Remember that you can change forms, but it can be difficult, and timing matters; so consult both an accountant and a lawyer if you plan to change forms after your initial choice.)

SOLE PROPRIETORSHIPS (NON-CORPORATE FORMS).

70% of all businesses are formed as sole proprietorships. These are best for self-employed individuals. Income and losses are treated as personal income for tax purposes and are filed using the individual's personal tax return. They are always on a calendar year basis, meaning that the business "year" begins on January 1 and ends on December 31. There is no limit to liability here; in other words, no shield from tort and other liability suits and no protection from creditors.

CORPORATE FORMS.

Many, however, prefer to incorporate to protect themselves from liability. That is the number one reason businesses incorporate. There is a limited to nearly-full liability shield for registered corporation owners that protects some or all non-stock personal assets of owners should the business default, or if there is a tort (personal injury or product or service liability) claim, depending on the corporate form chosen and the state in which it is formed. Delaware and Nevada provide stronger protections to the management of the business and to some extent to the shareholders as well, but all 50 states provide (usually through the office of the Secretary of State or Bureau of Corporations) registration capability for owners to incorporate. Of the choices, there are six legal forms which provide shields from liability to owners if they follow the "business judgment rule" (more on that later) and otherwise are prudent in their actions or are not personally responsible for the underlying cause of action against them. The shield? A big one! You can only lose your investment, not your home, savings, or retirement account.

The six legal forms are General Partnership ("**GP**"), Limited Partnership ("**LP**"), Limited Liability Partnership ("**LLP**"), Subchapter "C" Corporation ("**C-Corp**"), Subchapter "S" Corporation (either "**Sub-S**" or "**S-Corp**"), and Limited Liability Corporation ("**LLC**"). Each has a tax benefit or deficit that generally runs inverse to the amount of legal risk accorded to the business owner. Tax ramifications are that either income or losses are "passed-thru" to the owner's personal return(s) and taxed just like wages. In the case of C-Corps, taxes are only levied on dividends paid by the company after it is taxed first on its own income.

Prior to 1958 the only corporate forms that could be created were the C-Corporation, and General and Limited Partnerships. Limited Liability entities are relatively new; LLP's came into existence in the U.S.A. in the 1990's, while LLC's were first used in Wyoming in 1977, but did not start to appear elsewhere until the 1990's.

You should be aware that corporations are treated under law as entities with rights of "personhood" and share rights similar to those of people, such as the right to: bring a lawsuit, be taxed, get credit, protect their patents, trademarks, and copyrights, and have other benefits you and I take for granted.

Be also on notice that all corporations are registered at the state level, and not with the IRS or by the federal government. While you will have to get an EIN (employer identification number) or TIN (tax identification number) for your business from the IRS, only states register company entities. (You still file and pay taxes to both federal and state governments, however.) The benefits of registration bring with it tax responsibilities to the incorporating state as well as any other that you do business in. You will also need sales and use tax collection accounts and numbers and tax exemption certificates for purchases of goods you resell so you are not paying the tax to the state(s) twice. Finally, make sure you get all your permits and certificates from each jurisdiction in which you plan to do business, from the federal to the state to the county to the municipal level. Each wants their cut. (These taxes, filings, permits and registrations are required at all governmental levels regardless of the corporate form you choose.)

PARTNERSHIPS.

Somewhere between 10% and 15% of all businesses are one of three forms of Partnership. Note that in each case there must be a General Partner who is considered in charge and is the primary person of responsibility and liability; this is not the same thing as a General Partnership partner. General Partners are considered the legal designated liable partner under state incorporation laws. Every partnership must have a General Partner, even General Partnerships. (No puns intended.) Partners can leave by selling their partnership share. Many partnerships terminate when one or more partners leave by dying or retiring. There is no stock but each partner owns a specific percentage of the partnership and must claim that percentage of the annual profit or loss on their tax return yearly whether they want to or not. Those partners shielded from liability only risk losing their investment in the partnership.

General Partnership. General Partnerships are formed by two or more people who jointly and severally share ownership. They share profit and debt obligations as well as management and risk. Each can own an equal share or unequal shares. There is no restriction on the powers or authority of GP partners; each partner can sign for, and bind, the entire GP for any purpose and to any extent, without the approval of any other partners or even without a vote or notice. There is also no liability shield. Each individual partner is taxed on profits on their personal returns, but any losses can offset other income, subject to IRS tax regulations. The risk is that any partner can do anything and bind everyone. This creates a risk unless you know and trust ALL and not just some of your partners.

Limited Partnership. Limited Partnerships consist of two or more people, just like GP's, but with a difference: just one person is designated the General Partner and has more responsibility and more authority than the others. The partners that are not the General Partner are shielded from most liability (unless they clearly did "it") and usually only the General Partner is liable. Identically to that of a GP, LP partners are taxed as a pass-thru to their personal tax returns, and at individual rates.

Limited Liability Partnership. LLP's were created specifically for use by real estate investors and professionals such as attorneys and accountants, but are available to all. They provide additional tax benefits but are still treated as a pass-thru to the individual return. There is always one General Partner who is on the hook for liability and has superior powers to the rest of the partners. Not all states allow LLP's, but many do. The ability of each partner to have a liability shield against the misdeeds of another partner when they themselves are innocent is the driving force behind this kind of form.

CORPORATIONS.

Corporations make up the remainder (except for the above unincorporated Sole Proprietorships) of the forms of incorporation. A corporation can be called "Corporation" or Company" or "Inc." but all mean the same thing. (Each of these ending is called a "qualifier".) All publicly traded businesses are required by IRS regulations to be formed as a C-Corp. Others can form in any way they prefer but tax treatments are different. Corporations are not owned by partners, or even General partners, they have instead shareholders who own them and officers (employees) who run them. The liability shield is much more powerful but can still fail if a person is found to have broken the law or done something intentionally that caused the liability. Subchapter "C" and Subchapter "S" Corporations are so named for the section of the IRS code where they first appeared. Those shielded from liability by the corporation form only risk losing their investment in the company's stock, not their homes, cars, savings, IRS's, or freedom (e.g.: no jail).

Subchapter "C"-Corporation. A Subchapter C-Corporation is a separate legal entity that lives on even after the owner dies or sells out. This type of corporation must have stockholders who own the company, and employ officers who run it; the officers are chosen by a Board of Directors elected by the shareholders (usually the shareholders' only form of control). Non-employee shareholders have substantial immunity as they can only lose their stock value but face no other personal liability for any action of the corporation where they were not an employee or where they did not have personal authority to act. This is a powerful protection in that it shields "common" (every pun intended) shareholders who are not officers or employees from virtually all criminal or tort liability. Also, when a shareholder wants to exit, they merely sell their shares for the going market rate. Prior to 1958 there was no other corporate form other than a C-Corp.

Subchapter "S"-Corporation. Created by congress in 1958, the Subchapter S-Corporation provides all of the benefits and protections of the C-Corp but with taxation like partnerships. C-Corps are effectively double taxed because they tax first on income, and only from post-taxed income can dividends be then paid to the shareholders, which is then taxed again at the shareholder's personal income rate. But Sub-S "distributions" are taxed only once – on the individual owner's return – but at the regular wage income rates, unless it is denoted as a return on invested capital. S-Corp's do have limits, however. To agree to create this corporate form [*which Andrew likes best*] congress set some restrictions: S-Corporations can only be owned by individuals, not other corporations or partnerships; they cannot be owned by anyone who is not a U.S. citizen or a permanent resident alien residing in the United States, and there is a strict limit of 100 shareholders. (Some exceptions are made; estates, and certain trusts and non-profits can own shares under certain circumstances and if they are explicitly subject to and pay U.S. taxes on the income.)

Limited Liability Company (LLC)

LLC's are very similar to LLP's. They provide limited liability but with pass-thru tax treatment. They are "quasi-corporations" in the eyes of the states that allow them; they are not true corporations but provide the same benefits, liability shield, and other protections of a corporation but with partnership tax treatment for the owners. Instead of partners or officers, they have "Members." One Member is designated as the "Master Member" which is tantamount to being a General Partner but within a corporation instead of a partnership. The biggest disadvantage of an LLC is that profits may be subject to employment taxes (Social Security and Medicare) that can cost an additional 15.3% income, just as if you were self-employed. The biggest advantage of an LLC is that it can be formed with just one Member. There is no requirement, as in partnerships, that there be at least two owners; LLC's require only one.

HOW TO DECIDE ON YOUR CORPORATE FORM

Each corporate form has its merits and detriments.

C-Corporations are the bulk of what trades publicly in the stock market. These corporations have two distinct advantages but one expensive drawback. They provide a nearly impenetrable liability shield (far superior to any other business form) and allow public shareholders that include other companies and foreign entities and persons. However, they are "double taxed" which is to say that on their profits they first pay corporate income tax, and then the dividends they issue to stockholders is again taxed to the recipients at those peoples' individual tax rates. If you're publicly traded you need to be a C-Corp.

S-Corps are like partnerships, but with corporation status. They "pass-through" the tax rate so that profits are only taxed once, to the business owners. This income is proportional to the ownership percentage, and it is attributed whether distributed to the owners by dividend (or 'distribution') or not. This is the one problem with so-called "pass-thru" entities like S-Corps, LLC's, LLP's, and Partnerships. You pay income tax on the profits whether or not you have them paid to you, and you pay taxes every year. On the other hand, each of these pass-thru entities provides some form of liability shield, although the further you move away from corporations and toward partnerships, the less shield you have.

Sole Proprietorships are single or dual person businesses which are formed of just one person or a couple who are married (or otherwise legally bonded) who work together. Similar to the Unincorporated form, this offers very few protections. Unincorporated, where available, offers the least protection.

Joint Ventures are usually not recommended for most new ventures because they share both ownership and control, usually on a 50-50 basis, with a business partner. Their other investor or partner is an entity - a business. This is best for when each side has roughly half of a technology or asset base that if joined together into one venture, would provide synergies that would not exist if each side were to "go it alone" so to speak. Here, each side contributes roughly equal resources: money, time, technology, intellectual property, equipment, and so on, with the intent that they equally share the risk, and the rewards that flow from success.

And remember that there is always at least one person in every business form who cannot take advantage of that 100% shield.

In the case of LLC's, LLP's, and Partnerships, this would be the person in charge; the Master Member in the case of LLC's, and the General Partner in the case of Partnerships. In corporations, it is usually the CEO or President, or it's the owner if there is only one. In those cases, the only shield (but a powerful one) is to follow the "Business Judgment Rule." This provides some limited protection for any otherwise liable corporate actor if they act in the manner that a "reasonably prudent" person would act if in their position when making decisions for the company, and act in the interests of the company above any personal interests. This is also known as the Business Fiduciary Rule. Following this rule adds some shield protection to anyone who otherwise would be the at-risk person in charge. The problem is that the government wants someone to be responsible, and jailable, in the event of a criminal act.

Most businesses choose C-Corp or S-Corp status, but many professionals advise using LLC's if purchasing real estate or where the primary focus of the business is real property based. LLP's and Partnerships are best where there are one or more professionals who tend to group together, like lawyers, doctors, dentists, and accountants. Here, one person is in charge and that person is the General Partner or Master Member and they are responsible for the decisions, although any partner in a Partnership-type pass-thru business can legally make decisions. Only the "In-Charge" person is fully liable.

The most important thing is to choose some corporation form in order to take advantage of the liability shield, and to have a written, defined, and agreed-to-by-the-owner's resolution, charter, and operating agreement that has specific rules and procedures spelled out in writing. These operating agreements or "By-Laws" detail how the business will be organized, who the officers will be, the makeup of the board of directors and how many directors there will be, and other important rules for operating the business. This makes sure there are no surprises or problems when something needs to be done, as it is already clarified in the written rules. Then there are the classes of stock restricted in type and number for some corporate forms) and how that stock should be allocated among investors. (This will be covered later on when we talk about "Pitches" and second stage funding.)

While you can incorporate by yourself, it is better to hire a professional like a lawyer or a company that specializes in incorporations to do it for you. That way you don't make any mistakes, you don't miss doing something you should, and you take the guesswork out of the process. The fees above the actual incorporation costs are just a few hundred dollars extra at most per incorporation but they save many more dollars down the road if they prevent just one error in the incorporation process.

- - - -

HOW WILL YOU SET UP YOUR BUSINESS; WHERE WILL IT BE LOCATED?

The decision about how to set up your business is vitally important. The decision about where to locate your business is absolutely critical. Pick the wrong location and your business is as well as doomed from the start. "Just Beefburgers" won't fly in India.

There are many ways to set up your business which may also help with the location decision; they are popular and not impossible to facilitate. Consider the following three proven ways to do so:

AT HOME

What if you want to economize and setup an office in your home? Will you be interrupted by a pet or a family member while you are writing up an order or on the phone speaking to a customer? "Hey, keep my door closed!" Does that Sound familiar to those of you who have started to work at home?

For those of you who are thinking to start your own small business office, either out of necessity, being laid off from your present job, recently retired, or just plain burned out, think about working from home. When you get the itch to keep active or need the extra income, take the plunge into working from home. Home offices and home-based businesses require many things that traditional offices do not but end up costing allot less because you already have the location and do not need to rent an office. However, if you plan to take the home office deduction on your taxes, remember the rules from earlier in this chapter about making sure all things related to your business are used solely for your business and are not personal or the IRS will not only disallow your deductions but may come after you for penalties, interest, and possible jail time if you don't follow the rules.

In setting up an office in your home, you must prepare just as if you rent an office or buy a store elsewhere. You have to organize you time. You have to acquire the right supplies and equipment. You need funds (just not as much) and you need to know if you'll be doing business from your home.

There are a lot of benefits from working at home. The biggest benefit is that significantly shorter commute from your bed to your office chair.

Instead of miles, it's measured in feet. You get the advantage of low overhead costs since you don't generally pay yourself rent for the office part of the property. Oftentimes heat, electricity, and water are already there and you don't have to pay extra (although if you use a dedicated bifurcate-able space such as a garage of attached den you can set up separate electricity and phone lines). You end up paying, even with separate phone and other utilities, a lot less than you'd have to pay if you had to set up an outside office. Tax-wise, business expenses can be deducted on supplies, insurance and office space used in your home, as well as proportions for phone, Internet, electricity and heat if you can prove certain percentages of use by a log or other professional analysis. All these deductions are subject to keeping adequate records for IRS auditing. And you will get audited. The single highest audit rates are for people who claim home office deductions. Of course, you don't have to claim deductions for your home office; it will likely still be much cheaper than an outside office even if you don't. But you must make sure you have adequate, and separate from the rest of the distractions of the house, space to work in an <u>uninterrupted</u> work atmosphere.

(Yes, I'm overfocusing on that need to be interruption and distraction free, but with good reason.)

Investment wise, you will probably need one or more of each of the following separate, solely and exclusively dedicated-to-your-business items: a phone, desk, chair, computer, printer, office supplies (think paper, paper clips, staplers, pens and pencils, and the like), website and e-mail address, filing cabinets, storage boxes, a photocopier (unless your printer doubles as an inexpensive one that can handle high volume photocopying), scanner, cellphone (or use your own but this comes with its own risks) and signage. You will have to create an organized work schedule, with a specific time to start each day that you stick to. (You can't decide at 8:42 AM that you need an extra hour in bed.) You need to plan your day in advance, usually weeks at a time. You must also allot and calendar in time to read and reply to e-mail and regular mail, talk to prospects and customers (this should be done on a daily basis), and get your actual work done. Home offices do not mean lackadaisical hours or working "whenever I feel like it" but are the same as going to a real office but without the travel.

And dress the part. You should dress as if you were going into a real business office situated elsewhere. While you don't need to wear a suit (unless you are meeting with clients at this home office, which sometimes is a tax test for deductibility) you should not be in pajamas or underwear either. No sweatpants or t-shirts. Dress like you would if you worked for somebody else, in regular shirt and slacks or dress jeans. (There's some dispute as to if you should wear shoes or not; the general rule is YES if the home office is separate from the house or has a separate entrance or you meet clients there. But no flip-flops!)

And just because you work from home doesn't mean you shouldn't go out and network. On the contrary, it's now more, not less, important that you do so if you run your own business from your home because you are going to have less, not more, contact with people in a home office than an outside office. A good way to network is to be a "joiner" - local charities, non-profits, trade/networking groups like Rotary, Toastmasters, Church, social agency boards, the book club; are all good places to meet and share mutual experiences with each other. More specifically, business networking groups that call themselves Business Resource or Business Networking organizations are set up specifically to provide lead generation from one member to another. Some require each member to bring a lead for at least one other to every meeting, but some just act as meetinghouses and clearinghouses so that if you happen to know of a need you can say "I know a guy (or girl) through this group I belong to and they provide this (thing) that you need.

BUSINESS INCUBATOR PROGRAMS AND RELATED FACILITIES

Another possible location is as part of business incubator program. Similar to the "shared office" these operate as resource centers that also leases office and manufacturing space, usually below normal local rental rates, in a nice (and sometimes exceptional) work environment. These are shared offices or groups of offices where the office costs are shared; expenses for common services such as telephone answering and secretarial services and shared utility expenses lower everyone's individual overhead. Both start-up businesses and already established small businesses can take advantage of these locations. Low rentals for one or two years are offered to both small business startups and already existing small business manufacturing companies in many of these locations. Classic examples of such shared office businesses include professionals who need administrative services but not all the time; lawyers, accountants, and consultants are three of the best know examples of businesses that use incubator facilities.

The idea is to bundle all of the services together. This allows below market rental costs on leases, and lower overall costs per participant for shared common lobby and conference meeting rooms, janitorial services, building security, secretarial services, and Internet and computer access. Many of them either split the cost of the secretarial services or charge a low fee for phone call answering, word processing, photocopying, transcription services and after hour telephone message services. Because the biggest cost is usually the monthly service fee for non-salaried factors like electricity, Internet, and the like, the group only pays once for these recurring charges and so only needs to pay separately for used services. This does not lower the cost overall but lowers it dramatically on a per participant basis.

The advantage of incubator programs is that they also supply business services that can assist in financing, preparing business plans, relocation plans, and insurance counseling. In short, they have a consultancy built into the primary concept, and that provides invaluable assistance to small firms.

Typically, incubator programs have specific goals and objectives for the existing businesses and start-up small businesses that become their tenants. Usually geared towards the first year of life of a business, they sometimes provide service availability for two to three years depending on the business and their own ideology. For example, manufacturers in their second year of operation may be considered for an extension on their low-cost real estate leases if additional new jobs are created during that second year. Manufacturer tenants and/or existing small businesses then get an extension of one or two years on their leases. A mix of administrative and business products and services are geared to the needs of small business. The organizations SPDC and SCORE are available to help tenants develop business and finance plans, too. Advisory Committees generally oversee initial and ongoing operations, on what is usually a quarterly review of the status of each incubator's small businesses.

If you are a small business start-up or existing small business, see if your town or county has an incubator program and contact them for consideration and advice.

And don't forget the shared office, which has many of the same benefits but no limit on how long you can stay as long as you pay on time and don't ruffle your co-tenants' feathers. While rents may be at market, you can share one office in a building and pay much less for the rent and for the shared services - due to the shared aspect of the rental.

ENTERPRISE, EMPOWERMENT, AND STATE TAX-BENEFITTED ZONES

Then there are Enterprise Zones. Federal zones are called Enterprise Zones. States and localities have other names for their local versions, like Empowerment, Keystone, or Maine Pine-Tree Zone. All share the same advantages and disadvantages such as they are almost (but not always) located in the older inner-city industrial areas of major cities that need redevelopment and business to bring them back to life. They have myriad problems there, particularly crime, high unemployment, and usually significant cleanup costs. Many zones are created because surrounding neighborhoods have well-above average unemployment rates. A significant majority of these zones are in areas with above average low-income and minority populations. Most of these areas are run down, heavily gentrified, economically weak and contain primarily older, inefficient, multi-story buildings. Many streets need repair, infrastructure is old and poorly maintained, and they are usually strewn with used tires and trash and appear unattractive. The common theme in these zones is that before they were designated as zones it was extremely difficult or even impossible to get bank loans or other investment funds in these mostly red-lined areas.

All of this begs the question "(W)hy should I locate my small businesses HERE?)

How about a slew of benefits. Starting with reductions in taxes both on real estate and for sales tax. Paterson N.J. has such a zone and a Lowes, MEI Micro Center, and Pep Boys are located in it. Every one of these businesses is helped by the fact that sales taxes on goods and services purchased from and within the businesses in this zone are only taxed at half of the regular state sales tax rate. Pennsylvania and Maine (along with many other states) grant tax-incremental-financing, or TIF funding; this pays back to the business up to 85% of their state (and in some cases city) taxes (including payroll taxes) for hitting certain employment and investment goals, or maintaining certain investment or employment numbers over the 10-20 year life of the TIF period. Many TIF's are provided upfront, with credits against taxes due, to allow for companies to get some seed capital for their buildup in these zones.

So, what are the non-tax benefits? Low cost rent, for one. Retail stores, laundromats, workshops, and industrial and manufacturing companies all come because they get refurbished space at low rents. In turn they're expected to provide services to area residents... and jobs. It works both ways. Residents need jobs and cities need income so deals can be made. Financial incentives from lenders can foster economic development, reduce welfare and unemployment by bringing in new businesses to take advantage of these economic incentives. In the long run, both new businesses locating in enterprise zones and the local cities, state and federal governments will benefit. And the ultimate benefit from these zones, and their real purpose, is to bring in new jobs at average or above average pay, to local neighborhood people. In fact, a number of these zones require that at least a percentage of the hiring be of people who live within that town or city, and sometimes even within a measured distance from the zone itself. But it pays off for the business too in the form of people who want to work, and the goodwill it fosters in their new community from locals who are grateful they are there.

Small business owners, and lenders too, must have incentives to invest in the enterprise zones. Benefits like TIF's and other Tax abatements, tax credits to fix, expand or improve land and buildings, low interest loans for property purchases and improvements, security rebates, utility discounts, low interest loans on machinery and working capital for locating in the zone; these all help. Many locales offer loans for new equipment along with their city tax abatements. Employment training programs are available for job seekers and new hires of businesses within the zone, with incentives up to 50% of their salary covered by the municipality or state during the first two to six weeks on the job.

Contact your municipality's Commerce Department for information on any Enterprise Zones or local Zones in your area. It may be worth your while for the great savings you can get from being there, and the great reputation you can get from hiring there.

BUYING AN EXISTING BUSINESS FROM A RETIRING OWNER

Of course, not everyone wants to reinvent the wheel. Some owners grow tired of being in business. Maybe they're burned out. Maybe they're old and near, at or past retirement age and just want to cash out. Maybe they just died and the family has to sell to pay taxes or because they have no clue what the business does or how to run it.

When a person wants to sell a business, for any reason, it is important to understand what the driving force is behind the decision to sell. Each reason, business, and option is different, varied, and often both highly complex and irritatingly hard to draw out from the seller.

When buying a business, many buyers pay cash up front. But in most cases, unless that amount is ridiculously lower than what the business was truly worth, the odds are that sellers will only get a portion, a partial payment, up front, with the rest paid out over time. Many buyers hold back 10%-15% to ensure they get what was promised and the company performs as to the projections made by the seller before the sale. Some must pay off over time, like with professional services like attorneys, dentists, or landscapers. This is true where the price paid meets or exceeds one years' revenue.

Generally, buyers of going businesses offer a percentage of the money "down" with the balance paid over a period of months or years. Almost all buyers also want a transition period where the seller will assist for a time and make introductions to key suppliers and customers for the new owner. And most buyers will insist on a non-compete agreement to be signed by and bind the seller so they won't take the money and go right to work for a competitor or start anew and siphon off customers critical to the survival of the just-bought business. While many states do not enforce these agreements for employees, virtually everywhere does with respect to selling owners. They usually last as long as the payout time, but in some cases, may be lifetime bans (depending on how much the seller got and what the nature of the business is versus their expertise and contacts in that industry).

Let's imagine one. The owner is retiring. Maybe there's no family member to take over, or none are interested or even or capable of doing so. The business could be out-of-date (buggy whips?) or too demanding (24 hour on-call service). Long-term business prospects may look bleak. Perhaps special, specific skills may be required that family members do not possess. Or the owner may just not trust anyone, especially greedy relatives, to take over. It could also be that the owner is approaching or well past retirement age and is sick or incapacitated. Perhaps he's unrealistic as to what a buyer will pay.

The solutions here are to sell to an outsider or to liquidate the business's assets (and real estate) in order to cash out, so to speak. That is where you as a buyer step in. Of course, where there are partners, the remaining partner(s) may want to buy out the exiting partner's interest instead of selling to you.

But more on that later. Now on to Chapter 6, where we will cover how to Protect and Expand your business, and how to make your new nearly nothing into a viable something.

CHAPTER SIX
Protecting and Expanding Your Business

PROTECTING WHAT YOU PROCREATE

A funny thing about copycats is they come in both the non-profit and for-profit types. Many copycats imitate their competitors, so stealing ideas or products not only happens between big businesses, but among small businesses too. I know, because it has happened to some of my friends, and it also happened to our initial start-up business of making steel table slides.

When you have a creative quality product or a great new idea you have to make sure that it is hidden "below the radar" and not easily visible to your competitors or else is protected prior to launch. Otherwise, it is going to be copied by copycat competitors. Of course, once you market your product or service, it is already out there and you have no shield. But prior to that, or during the initial rollout phase, low-key helps to prevent competitors from swooping in to copy your product or service, and steal your customers. It also is important to protect your ideas through registration. The best way that successful people accomplish this is by taking steps to protect themselves and their new creations and works is through the registration their intellectual property in the form of patents, copyrights, trademarks and trade dress.

Patents and copyrights are protected pursuant to Article 1, Section 8, Clause 8 of the United States Constitution: "To promote the Progress of Science and useful Arts, by securing for limited Times to Authors and Inventors the exclusive Right to their respective Writings and Discoveries." The terms of protection have changed in length over the years; most patents are now protected for either 14 or 20 years, with some exceptions. Note that the protection granted by a patent is mostly one of prevention: it allows you to prevent others from duplicating your product for the specified patent protection period. You never have to make your product or sell your product, but you can keep others from doing so as well. The America Invents Act, signed by Barack Obama on September 16, 2011, switched U.S. right to the patent from the previous "first-to-invent" system to a "first-inventor-to-file" system for patent applications filed on or after March 16, 2013. If you want to protect your product or invention by patent, you must file a patent application as soon as possible, but always within. The three primary types of patents are Utility, Design, and Plant patents. To be patentable, it must have Novelty (newness; non-obviousness), Utility (it has to do something; it must be "useful"), and Inventiveness (the first of its kind). Patents do not protect written words or thoughts. Written word protection is provided by copyright. While copyright cannot and does not protect ideas themselves (nothing protects ideas) the copyright protects the order and format of those ideas; the work is copyrightable when it is written in a specific format, like the words in this book. The idea of a business plan is not copyrightable, but the way (we) wrote this book and the order of the ideas as they appear on the pages, is. Facts cannot be copyrighted, but whimsical stories can. Copyrights last a lot longer; for anything you create after January 1, 1978, the length of protection is either: your life plus 70 years (70 years after the last author dies), or 95 years (from first publication), or 120 years from creation, whichever one is shorter, but subject to a minimum of 25 years of protection regardless. Earlier creation was subject to different time rules. (If prior to 1978 and not published or registered, the 70/95/120 lengths apply but with an overriding guaranteed protection until at least December 31, 2047, other factors notwithstanding.) (U.S. Copyright Office, Circular 15A, 2011.)

Trademarks (and trade dress) are also protectable. These are available solely to operating businesses. Trademarks are symbols or names or words or colors or sounds that identify your product. (Think Coca-Cola and the shape of the bottle, Nike's swoosh, Apple's half eaten apple, and the sound NBC makes at the beginning of a show when the NBC Peacock appears onscreen and there are three chimes.) Trademarks identify your business or product and are only protectable so long as you continue to use them in commerce. Trade dress is the term for how the business or product looks instead of a symbol for it. Trade dress might be the color and design scheme of Red Lobster restaurants, or the 7-Eleven store logo. All of these are forms of "Intellectual Property." Intellectual Property (or "IP") is, in general, any product borne of human intellect that the law protects from unauthorized use by others. Patents and other protections are how an inventor can register their creation with the government to protect it from use or misuse by unauthorized persons.

While these protections are important, they do not protect from everything. Especially when someone copies your work in just a different enough way to circumvent these protections and compete with you anyway. But not all ideas need to be protected. Some just need to be put into practice and "let fly."

MARKETING MATTERS

Merriam-Webster's dictionary defines "Marketing" as: "(T) he act or process of selling or purchasing in a market; (T)he process or technique of promoting, selling, and distributing a product or service."

A manufacturer of men's pants was a good example of a successful small businessman who had an idea that started a new way of merchandising. His idea was to sell the pants by mail order, through small ads in consumer magazines. At the time it was an original and unique way of marketing in the retail clothing trade. (Today everyone does it, whether by catalog or online.) But as his business grew nationwide, he sold his pants through his own direct retail outlets, too. That way, he could get both channels of business: mail order and "brick-and-mortar" walk-in. His then-novel idea to do something different than others by selling through mail order proved successful. You must keep ahead of the curve in competition. The pants man did it by placing small ads listing special pants sizes that just a select group of people needed but that were unavailable or difficult to find in competitor's clothing stores, before he started his niche advertising gambit, which paid off handsomely.

Marketing continues to change today. Most marketing now occurs through television or online through portals such as Facebook or Google, and is becoming less dependent on newspapers and magazines… and direct mail, which is still the best way to reach people. Online sales in 2018 were about 10% of total domestic retail sales in the Unites States, up from around just 7% in 2015. This number is growing fast, thanks to companies such as Amazon. Internet sales may be more profitable in the future, should companies find a solution to the ever-rising cost of shipping. Most successful small businesses sell products or perform services to a narrow, specific market segment, that they hope others can't meet the needs of. So, if a company can promote what they do well and get potential customers to know they exist and offer them a better solution to their problems or a perfect product for their needs, they can succeed just like the pants man did.

To be successful, you must have ambition and desire not to quit in the face of risk. You have to have a passion to sell your product, as well as know your strengths and weaknesses. And you must have a plan – a good plan – as to how you will reach your potential customer and how you will market to them once you do.

Small Businesses look for unique ways to merchandise and we wanted to do so, too. They oftentimes get ideas from other industries or mediums. Let me give you a contemporary example.

Imagine an entertainer who specialized in the unusual. Most of the audience for his shows were baby boomers. The entertainer specialized in "covering" songs that the great "Velvet Frog" - Mel Torme - had sung when he was alive. (Torme died in 1999 at the age of 73.)

This particular singer captivated the audience with almost 20 Torme-like renditions, including "Mountain Greenery," "Lula's Back in Town," and "Blue Moon." The crowd was enthusiastic, and cheered both the songs, and the singer. After the show was over, the singer mingled in the audience and pitched his own compact discs for sale, which contained more than a dozen of the Torme songs he'd just performed. Smart, great merchandising. A double hitter. He was getting paid for entertaining these people, by these people, and he also was marketing his CD's of the songs he'd just sung for them: songs just performed in the show. This entertainer had discovered a niche, and filled it, and made money from both ends at the same time. A true entrepreneur!

Small Businesses that are just starting out, or revamping, or even doing an alternative to their present marketing operations, should take a page out of that singer's book and use a novel marketing technique.

Small Businesses need to reflect on ways to change directions in what they do, to seize the opportunity to do something different and unique, and to do things that are not being done but have met success in the past or that otherwise could be used to fill a special need again, even with changes in technology.

Small Businesses have to look for goods or services needed that are not presently supplied, or not been successfully used but that could be popular again. It could be profitable to a small business even where it was no longer profitable to a large company. Some products or services could produce big profits on a small volume scale by a small business to a select market, after their success fades with big companies in a large nationwide market. It is all about opportunities and moving fast in a fast-moving world.

So how do you market your company's newest product or idea when there is already so much clutter? In 1900 virtually 100% of ad dollars were spent in print publications. In 2018 about 40% of all worldwide advertising dollars were spent on online ads. That's 40 cents out of every dollar! And online now appears to rule. Or maybe not.

For hundreds of years newspapers ruled the advertising roost. Magazines followed in the late 1800's. In the 1920's radio appeared, and in the 1940's television began to broadcast. Billboards soon followed. Each successive format just complimented the earlier ones, and all thrived. Then came the Internet and the age of online advertising in the late 1990's. Now newspapers that used to publish 100 pages daily and hundreds of pages on Sundays are lucky to have 24-48 pages daily and maybe 60-100 pages on a Sunday. Ad volume (and dollars) in newspapers have dropped over 50% just in the last 10 years. Some of this is due to consolidation in the retail trade (Macy's contains remnants of several dozen acquisitions such as Marshall Field's, Wanamaker's, Gimbels, and May's) and with such consolidation comes fewer companies to insert ads. Other retailers are out of business (Toys-R-Us, Circuit City, Gymboree, Bon-Ton, Payless ShoeSource) and their ads simply disappeared. Many advertisers have abandoned newspapers altogether as not timely enough; they have gone over to "the dark side" – the Internet. Magazines have suffered a similar fate. Many have halted publication, and those remaining are "thinner" and printing fewer pages due to fewer ads being bought to show to their diminishing readers, in an ever-repeating and vicious downward spiral. Newsweek, U.S. News and World Report, Playboy, and Glamour and all examples of magazines that eliminated print editions in favor of online-only editions. With fewer ad pages, many publications, some of which have published for over a century, are now gone or are going away.

Direct mail has been around almost as long as the Post Office. The USPS delivered 146.4 billion items in 2018, of which 77.3 billion were marketing items. This was the best way to reach someone, since the USPS delivers to nearly 160 million addressees a day. While first class mail has been dropping in volume over the years as more people pay or receive bills online and send e-mails instead of letters, the USPS probably still reaches more people and delivers more ads that actually get read than any other method. (Many people tend to ignore online ads unless they are search results.) And yet direct mail may not be the best option for some as many direct mailings are considered "junk mail" and are disposed of without being read. [*But direct mail still works. I look through the "marriage mail" inserts each week and occasionally buy things from some of them.*]

Television is suffering the same fate, but slower. As recently as the early 1980's there were only four choices: the "broadcast networks" of ABC, CBS, NBC and non-commercial PBS (Public Broadcasting). Now there are literally hundreds of cable and digital broadcast channels, and that's not including so-called streaming services such as Amazon, Netflix, Hulu, Roku, YouTube, and others. Each is fighting for their share of dwindling broadcast advertising dollars that are also split among so many different venues - and a person can only watch for so many hours in a day. Then of course there is the online website, or portal. This new type of advertising venue takes the form of Google, Facebook, Yahoo, Twitter, Pinterest, Instagram, and literally millions of others. There are estimates that in 2012 there were more than 600 million active websites, and that in 2019 there will be as many as ONE BILLION active websites. The first online ad, a banner added to a webpage, was posted on October 27, 1994. Nowadays each person is exposed to (or tortured into seeing) somewhere between 4,000 and 12,000 ads per day, with the average being 5,000 per day according to marketing firm researcher Yankelovich, Inc.

And they ain't cheap. In 2017, Facebook's revenue was over $40 billion dollars, and Google's revenue was over $110 billion dollars. Most of this revenue was from display, search, or other advertising shown on their websites. That's more than television, which had just $42 billion dollars of 2017 national broadcast advertising revenue. Together, Facebook and Google alone account for more than 40% of all online advertising dollars. Yeek!

But is Internet advertising best for your business? It depends on whom you are trying to reach. Newspapers and direct mail still reach those who will not or cannot rely on or use Internet technology, such as the Amish or many rural farmers and others who have insufficient or non-existent Internet. Television reaches more people at one time, but at a high cost, and then usually only during major events such as sports league playoffs or one-off or one-time events such as awards shows.

Internet, like e-mail, can be targeted specifically to narrow groups of people, but tend to get ignored. Only Internet search results are guaranteed to be viewed, but this really only works if someone already knows to look for your product or service and you hope they find you instead of a competitor, which can cost significantly per "click" on your business name from the search results. Of course, you can use a web-portal so sell your goods such as Amazon, Apple, or E-Bay, but these vendors make money by not only charging you to list your goods through them, but take a cut of the sale as well.

So you must know to whom you are marketing, how you want to reach them, what you are willing to pay for your "lead" and be able to make a good guess as to if the intended viewer will actually see your ad and respond to it. And there are no guarantees they will respond. But you must have a marketing plan or you're unlikely to get any business at all.

- - - -

You have to love what you do, especially to start your own Small Business. What makes a person want to be in business? Money? Fame? The independence of being your own boss? Could be all three.

Many people ask me "How did you get in business?" How indeed. I tell them I researched what I wanted to do, and I spent lots of time reading up on the types of businesses I was interested in. I had to choose whether to be a part-timer or a full-timer. I asked myself "where would I locate my office (or plant)?" I had to choose whether it was in, or out, of the city. Did I need a partner or outside financing or could I finance it myself? All of these plus the oftentimes staple "I saw an opportunity and it was too good to pass up" helped determine my answer to the asker. And you will need to answer all of these things, too.

Actually, and I've said this a number of times before, including earlier in this book, it would be smart to first work for a company that does the things you would like to do, before you start headlong into your own company. Often times the best source of a new business is an old hobby. Many people grow a hobby into a business, or have experience in a specific trade that determines their direction. Both are good ways to begin thinking about what you want to, and actually can, do in your own new business.

Here is a good example: many years ago, a bookstore owner was asked by a young law student what was really needed in his business. The bookstore owner replied "Why doesn't someone make the law library bookcases out of steel instead of wood?" The fact was that some bookcase shelving was already made of metal for libraries, in a limited amount. But no one exploited it.

Yes, the law student saw a void to be filled. So, he and his brothers, who had a small metal fabrication shop, did just that. They looked into making metal law library bookcase shelving. As a result, they built a small mom and pop business, and turned an idea into a livelihood, and a successful business.

Of course, it's not easy. Present trends have to be "bucked" and old-school customers need to be convinced that the new product is really a "new way" and a benefit to them beyond what they get from their current suppliers and product purchases. Designing, fabricating, and pricing a new product for future sales is tough because there is no prior entrant with your new product to show you the way forward, the potential for your product, and how to market it. In competing against wood products, steel has to show how it is either cheaper, better, or both. It had to be painted or it would rust, so different paint colors had to be added. Various metal thicknesses were considered as to what was the proper weight bearing capacity and requirements for the weights of books loaded on each shelf. Then, how was it to be delivered intact with no dents or damage? Corrugated packaging was needed to make sure the shelving arrived in pristine condition, without scratches or any damage to the unit itself. All of these concerns cam about by investigating how to sell just one product for one purpose. (Although, many purposes would eventually show themselves later on.)

So, each brother in the business took a separate task. One was an engineer, another had a financial accounting background, and the third had both law school and business school marketing and management training. Each one was suited to a specific component of the management of the business - from engineering, to production, to finance, to marketing, to management, to sales. They worked tirelessly every day from dawn to dusk, with a passion to succeed. Each did their part by specializing in what each knew best, and using that skill to do their part of the whole of making the business succeed.

This metal shelving was engineered efficiently and correctly. It filled a niche. It was quality made and priced right to sell in the marketplace. Once this product became successful with law and other libraries, it was adapted with modifications to sizes, thicknesses (Gauge) and colors to sell to other buyers for use in other business, and eventually consumer, applications. Business continued to flourish, with sales to large companies and even major retailers and distributors in the grocery, automotive and electronics industries. They had "arrived" in the marketplace. But they felt the need to do better. So, they did.

Business is built on three main cornerstones: price, reliability, and trust. Pricing must be reasonable; your product does not have to be the cheapest nor the most expensive but it must be priced fairly for the product. Reliability is paramount even over price: a product or service MUST deliver the benefits it promises; if it fails to do so, no one will buy it again. Trust is earned and comes through constantly and consistently providing the promised benefits of the product or service and sometimes even exceeding them without raising price. Delivery is also part of trust; it must be delivered ON TIME or it will be the Last Time it is sold to that customer because customers hate late deliveries. Especially late deliveries of critical products.

[Let Andrew tell you about how trust really works:

I was working in the business all through college. The usual routine was I would go into the steel warehouse and open up around 7:30 AM, make sure everything was running smoothly, then go out with my father about 8:30 for a quick bite of breakfast. At 9:00 when the caller window opened, we would pick up the mail from the post office. One morning about 8:00 A pickup truck pulls up. A man, who appeared to be Amish or Memmonite, got out and asked about roofing sheets we were offering for sale through an ad in the classified section of the paper. I took him and his two children on a tour (in safer areas) of most of the plant and showed him the more than 25,000 steel sheets we had on the floor. He wanted to check the quality and pricing in person. So I showed him. It took nearly an hour. He bought 10 sheets for I believe it was $7.50 each. Then my father, who was running late that morning, came by for our morning trek. We usually went to a small hole-in-the-wall diner – which usually have the best food – with a $.99 special for eggs, bacon toast and coffee. We invited these customers along. After breakfast he thanked me and said "you know you spent a lot

119

of time on us today and yet we only bought 10 sheets from you." I said "My position is that you're a customer. I treat customers the same whether they buy 10 or 10,000 sheets, and that's with courtesy." He and his two kids then got in his station wagon and drove home.

A few weeks later, about 10 in the morning, two massive 48' flatbed trucks pulled up and parked along the side street in front of the plant. A man got out of the first truck cab carrying two large paper bags. It was the same man. He asked me if I remembered him. In a funny truth, I had been thinking about him for some reason that morning and said "Yes your name is ---- and I remember you bought 10 sheets of roofing. He then said "do you remember what you said" and I said Yes, and then repeated my mantra about how I treat customers. I had a reputation for providing that kind of care to customers that was well known in our industry. Then he took the two bags and emptied them onto the center of my desk.

Up to that point in my life I had never seen $25,000 in cash. I got scared. Then he said "someone who took the time to help me, even for a little purchase, had to be honorable, and someone who went to a $.99 breakfast had to be frugal, and someone who is willing to make a deal on price for a bigger order is smart. I can do business with you." And he did annually for nearly 10 years, until I left to pursue my MBA and we sold the business. And always bought at least as much, at the best price I ever offered anyone. You can't make this stuff up; it's all true!]

That story remained with Andrew all these years. He learned that if you treat customers with integrity and respect, they come, and they come back. Word of mouth and reputation are how companies grow. "Fair dealing" must become your Golden Rule, and will instill trust in your customers.

So over the years the shelving business grew from a very small 4,000 sq. ft. space to nearly half-a-million square feet of manufacturing, packing, and shipping facilities. That growth took time, and was the result of customers repeat buying because the business kept promising, and delivering on those promises.

This was a single idea, to make a product out of steel instead of wood. But it grew beyond that. The result was a micro-business that grew into a giant operation because of a single good idea. Often is heard the maxim that to succeed a person needs to be the most educated or most talented, but that just isn't always the case. The hardest worker often gets the most success. Another maxim is that the bigger the investment the better the chances. That may often be a truism, but not in most cases. Again, people can be successful with an idea if they marry that idea with hard work and a strong business plan. Remember: only about 20% of all new businesses are still around five years later. Sometimes it is luck, but that's the ten-percent. The other 90% is always hard work.

"90% Perspiration and 10% Aspiration."

So how do you ensure that your business is one of those 20 Percent?

Start with a solid and comprehensive written business plan. This shifts some of the odds in your favor. Business plans are essentially road maps of what your mission is; what products or services you intend to sell, where and how will you market, how you intend to finance the business, the personnel you need to operate it, and where you will physically locate your business.

You don't have to run more than one business to be successful. Money alone doesn't always drive people (but it is a good indicator of success; it's very useful to pay your bills). Getting a great feeling doing what you do is what counts even more. It takes long hours and a commitment to finish the task that makes successful small business people. The challenge is to do what you like to do, with integrity, gusto and drive.

"Work Hard, Play Hard. Every Day, In Every Way." This is what my father told me all the time. He always focused on doing the work necessary, and whether work or play to give it your all. I know I keep focusing on the hard work aspect, but that is really the single most important thing in making your business successful. Many well-capitalized businesses fail because they have the money, they have the idea, and they have the "wherewithal" to get thing done, but they never do. The owner slacks off or figures "I don't have to be there to watch it or run it I can just invest and sit back and let the money come to me." That's the best way to fail. You have to believe in what you do. And you have to do the work. And work is not really work when you enjoy doing it. In the end you can accomplish your wildest dreams. It is never too late to start your own small business. Like I tell my son (when he's not helping me to write this book) "I never actually worked a day in my life because I always loved what I did" [*and his son, the co-author, will confirm that his father actually says this all the time*].

- - - -

Let's go back and revisit the steel table slide business. We had started up two small businesses; one the manufacturing of steel table slides, the other, a partnership with two other companies to assemble kitchen dinette sets for the furniture resale trade. Now we went into a third business: the manufacture of steel shelving for use by other businesses. We chose to manufacture the shelving in the same factory building as the other two businesses and at the same time. This would allow us to use fallow time during production sops to make other products, so we would be more fully utilizing our facilities, personnel, and resources. This is now called productivity but then was just called prudent. Late on the shelving company would grow into a multi-line business servicing commercial, retail, wholesale, manufacturing and real estate trades. In other words, over time, it went from being a small idea to being a big success.

So, as I said before, each of us had a specific responsibility in our business. One took care of the office operations, one oversaw the three manufacturing groups, and one focused on sales and marketing. It was a full-time job for six people overseeing all three ventures at once, but the three of us put in the extra hours and made it a success. It grew and became bigger because we put in the effort.

Orders continued to grow both in size and in dollars at an amazing rate for the new shelving business. After the first year there was a natural progression to see other uses for this limited shelving line, which was becoming less and less limited. Some of the new applications, however, were for things we didn't make. Thus, we made use of a new type of business, that of being a "jobber" of goods. "Jobbed" or relay-sales of products are goods that are sold by a manufacturer but which they do not themselves make. Manufacturers sometimes do this to "fill out" their line of products so that they appear to carry a full line when in fact they don't make a full line. For a shelving manufacturer, this could take the form of metal desks and work benches, slotted angle bars, steel storage cabinets, steel drawer units (which we later made ourselves) and lockers (which we also later made ourselves).

Such "jobbed" (bought from outside manufacturers but sold as if we made it ourselves) products are usually ordered from another manufacturer but shipped by that other manufacturer under the primary business name: an example is Company A sells a widget, but needs to sell wodgets too. If they make widgets but not wodgets they order wodgets from Company B and Company B ships the wodgets to Customer C but with paperwork and marking and labels that say Company A on them. This makes it look to Customer C like Company A made the wodgets as well as the widgets, when in fact they don't make both. This is "jobbing" and "drop-shipping" (we discussed this earlier) and fills out an otherwise streamlined product line. These products might also be shipped by the outside supplier directly to our facility where they would be stripped of their original identification and repackaged and private labeled by us to ship under our own name. Then afterwards, we shipped or drop-shipped those products to our distributors (or directly to their customers in the distributor's name as shipper just as had been done for us).

But we weren't selling enough of those jobbed products at that time to warrant spending the money to acquire and set up the tooling, dies, and materials needed to make those items ourselves. For those items we did see enough critical mass of sales for we did eventually go into making ourselves. Meanwhile, several non-competitor manufacturers were glad to sell us those products that we didn't make ourselves, as much for the business as for the fact we did not compete with them. Years later, when our sales volume increased on those items, we started to manufacture those products ourselves.

PROFIT MARGINS AND PROFITABLE PERFORMANCE

One of the most critical questions to be answered by a new business is "how do I price my product (service) and how high can I price it and still not lose sales? This is the magic question for every business since the dawn of business time. How to price could take up a whole book (and still not help much) but some things are basic: price close to market, and unless you provide something extra with your product like faster delivery or a better performance, don't price above the market. Only price below the market if you can still at least break even (and then only for a short promotional time) so that you don't price yourself into bankruptcy. Pricing depends on several factors, including knowledge of how much the market will bear, what your costs are, and how much profit you need (or want) on a per-item basis.

Most businesses use some form of marketing promotion such as coupons, BOGO's (buy-one-get-one free or at a reduced price for the second one) and lowball sales gimmick pricing for short periods, such as the opening day or week. Retail is more likely to require such promotional pricing "gimmicks" than manufacturing (where delivery and consistency is more important than a super low intro price). For most retailers, a low introductory price will get people into your store to try the product and hopefully like it enough to repeat. Sales and promotions are used to get people to try, not to repeat buy. The single hardest thing for a retailer or retail manufacturer to do is to wean consumers off of discounts.

But most businesses (and those that want to succeed) use a centuries-old formula that still works to this day (with some exceptions) that goes: "A Third A Third and A Third." That is: attribute 1/3 of your wholesale price (not retail but your cost to make) toward labor, 1/3 toward material, and 1/3 toward overhead. Where the percentages must shift due to the individual mechanics of the specific business (like a labor-intensive business is more than 1/3 labor) then you must tinker and adjust the formula as it applies to your specific business. It does, however, apply in many businesses. In many cases, however, the formula is really sixths. Roughly evenly split between labor, rent, overhead, materials, production costs, and logistics and handling costs.

But "correct" pricing can take another form, "markup" - setting a price high enough that after all of this is done you make a profit. This formula is also a historical one: markup from cost to sales price is somewhere between 50% and 100%. The empirical example of this is a product, say a widget, that has a variable cost ("variable cost" is the cost to make one more item; "fixed cost" is the cost of running the facility whether you make 1 or 100,000 pieces) $1.00 to make. $.30 labor per part, $.60 material per part, and $.10 for utilities and paint, for example. To cover overhead, fixed cost, and allow for a reasonable profit, this $1.00 widget should be sold by the manufacturer for between $1.50 and $2.00 per piece to the manufacturer's immediate customer. Your customer can then mark it up as they see fit for sale to their (or the final) customer(s). (An example: supermarkets use a normal markup. Sam's Club, a division of Wal-Mart, marks up products only 16%-20% from their cost and not 50%-100% like most regular retailers.)

Back to our steel business. Our original markup on jobbed products was 25% above the distributor's net cost price to us. Once we were making these products ourselves, our profit markup was higher - 40% above our fabricating costs instead of 25%, which gave us more in profit on our return-on-investment and thus increased our profits on those items. As we continued to expand our distributor base, we added Manufacturers Representatives to sell our products to each of the distributor trades. This allowed us to expand our sales without having to expand our sales costs.

We had jobbed steel garment industry equipment to buyers like sewing machine dealers, who also sold our shelving products to end users like men's clothing and women's apparel companies. We jobbed a line of steel felling troughs, box trucks, garment stands and clothing tub containers that opened the door to sell our steel shelving along with those jobbed items for the garment industry makers.

The owner of the company that made these garment industry products that we bought for resale was an elderly owner-operator, with four employees. We made arrangements to have him ship the garment equipment products we sold to our distributors for their sewing and garment industry customers.

We shipped shelving orders in his name to his customers and he gave us the same courtesy on drop-ship orders to our own distributors. It was a mutually beneficial deal. In return, we were selling him our steel shelving and we drop-shipped in his company's name to his sewing and garment industry customers.

After the elderly man's heart attack, he asked us if we would make these items for him, on an exclusive and protected basis, so we did. We began to manufacture his products for sale solely in his company's name in a three-state region, for sales only to his accounts in his name. We, in return, would sell his products to our distributors outside those three states. We both agreed to, and honored, these terms and conditions for our mutual benefit. This is how we became familiar with the concepts of custom manufacturing, and exclusive territories.

We hired two of his skilled workers to work on his product lines at our plant. We paid the owner for his machinery so we could take over manufacturing for him (and for us) and this arrangement lasted for more than five years until he finally retired. Subsequent to that event, we were allowed to sell to his dealers and we could not sell anywhere, without regional restrictions.

We now had 26 full-time paid employees, not including ourselves. Our sales volume increased so much in the steel shelving end of the business that we encountered another concept: limited capacity. We had to make a choice (and we chose) to discontinue making the steel table slides that started our business. Out three-way partnership in the dinette business was ended and we now focused 100% on the manufacturing and sales of steel shelving. Things were changing, and so were we, apparently.

Our sales representative that covered national retail buyers didn't want to use telephone solicitations to market our storage shelving products for resale to the retail store trade. He was a hands-on guy who preferred to visit in person and directly worked with buyers from large chain stores. When he visited one particular such store, what he learned about their standard buying procedures "blew his mind" so to speak. The buyer that he contacted specialized in-home storage product sales, and insisted on knowing our company dollar sales volume for the past two years. This was so he could determine if we had sufficient capacity to produce extra-large orders, such as the one they contemplated. One specific product was picked and net prices were provided (discounts or net prices made the price lower per item when the volume rose). Lead times on different orders and their shipment times were requested. Then, the buyer had our factory inspected to ascertain the quality of the product and the factory's capabilities of meeting specific shipment delivery dates to its various store locations.

This was a smart buyer in the role of a purchasing agent. We were a capable producer with the product to sell and the right price to sell it. But we had no clue as to what volume of monthly orders would be made by the retailer. All our representative could tell us was that they wanted to market one of our products using three different pricing techniques, and we were being considered as a provider if we could prove we could produce on time and at price. How could the retailer sell only one model yet bring in sufficient profits, we asked? The retailer wanted to market the one product using three different price techniques. It was a simple idea; so simple in fact that one could overlook the answer.

The buyer ordered it in three colors: black, white, gray. It was so simple it would be a born moneymaker for the retailer. All they had to do was differentiate the price by the color: in displays the black unit was priced at, say (in today's dollars) $49.95, the gray one at $59.95 and the white one for $69.95.

What were they thinking? Was there any logic in selling the identical product (other than the color) at three different prices? Would a consumer know the only difference was the paint color?

But the retailer already knew the answer. Twenty-five percent of all buyers bought at the cheapest price regardless of the color because they wanted the lowest price due to their budget. So promotions that showed various colors and different prices levels per color were made to entice different types of customers. Next, he said "over 50% of the customers bought the middle-priced product because they don't want to buy the cheapest one nor the most expensive one."

The final 25% of consumers will buy the highest priced one because of a perception that the higher price equates with the best quality; they are willing to pay more for it even if something nearly identical is available for less money. Scientific marketing at its best to be sure for the seller, but not for the end user. But we learned a tremendous lesson from it. While we agreed that it was unfair to the buyer, it is highly beneficial to the seller. And what's fair and what's not depends on your point of view. But we were able to glean an important trust from this: people will pay more when they perceive more benefit from it. Faster delivery, higher quality, something exclusive... give the customer something beneficial and extra and they will pay a higher price for it.

Remember, you can learn from your customers too, just like we did! Growth and profit are there for the taking, it just takes insight and work (and a bit of luck).

Next, we ventured into office furniture, as a natural progression from what we were making. A leading office furniture reseller near us sold lots of our shelving. We were their biggest single supplier. Then they went bankrupt. They owed lots to many, including us. The owner, who knew and trusted us, thought we could rescue his company. So he offered us an opportunity: take over ownership of his company while he continued to manage operations. As the largest creditor, this might work, we thought. And we had his expertise because he was staying on, but we would benefit from ownership.

It was a make-or-break decision for us, and for him, since we only sold to resellers and if we screwed up it would likely cause the furniture business to fail again, for good. But we took that risk; to recoup the monies owed to us, and to take a risk on a business that could make us far more successful if we made it work. It was a substantial and highly risky decision at that time, with great upside by nearly fatal repercussions for failure. So we did it. The retailer had top-tier office furniture, some exclusively. We gambled and we made a good decision because he ran it properly and we made big money from their sales. However no "sure thing" is perfect, and we saw trouble brewing with the office staff and sales personnel. We came upon a choice that all business owners have to make at some point: choose your path when faced with two diverging business opportunities. Andrew was once in a business with a partner who wanted to make a widget and run the malls that sold them. The question was did his partner want to be a widget seller who also ran malls or a mall operator who also made widgets?

We saw the handwriting on the wall and realized we could continue the retail side of the business but it would draw us away from our manufacturing operation. The latter was more profitable and we would have more control over it. So here, the choice was easy. Keep the manufacturing, sell the retailer.

Why this path? Several of our shelving business customers stopped buying from us. When I asked why, they told me that we were now in competition with them. What did we need to do, I asked, so that they would buy from us again? To a one they all answered that we should close the stores or sell them. Then they would buy from us again.

Remember that "A Third A Third A Third" rule? Well in retailing, labor can be up to 50%, not 33%. Record keeping is costly, and accountants and lawyers are necessary not optional. We decided that it was better to make than to retail, and once we closed the retailer six of the seven dealers who saw us as competition earlier started buying from us again. The old lawn mower business axiom of giving 100% to your own business was the right thing to do and it proved the point for us, to sell to dealers and not to end users.

We once again succeeded by following our one simple rule: stick to your business plan, and success should follow you wherever the road takes you.

We manufactured many additional products that complimented our focus on steel products, such as a patented shelving line, racks like those in Costco or Sam's Club to store heavy products on, supermarket gondola shelving, lockers to store clothing and schoolbooks in, and even steel formed sheets that we corrugated and made roofing out of. For 40 years we ran our ever-enlarging business until we reached out own retirement points. (Let me point out that the Author has failed retirement numerous times, including by writing this book.) Once my brothers decided to retire, we decided to sell the business.

PRIVATE LABELING

Sometimes you grow not by making your own products but by making someone else's. Think of basically every store-brand product. Stores don't own plants that make paper towels, spaghetti, detergent, and aspirin. Private labeling keeps literally hundreds of thousands of Americans working, and with good reason: lots of people can't or won't afford brand name products. Every time you buy a bottle of detergent, Ibuprofen bottle, or O's Cereal, one of the things written in small print at the bottom of the back of the label will be "not manufactured by P&G" or "not manufactured by Unilever" or "not made by General Mills". And yet many products are. Private labeling is all the more important to understand because many brand names make private label products but must disclaim to protect their own brands.

You can do this too and make good money even if you sell for a close margin over cost. Volume makes a big difference in what is formally called "contract manufacturing" for others.

We did it. We had made a packaged shelving unit for sale through a top 10 U.S. retailer. They wanted their name on it, however. They paid us enough to do it so we made a profit on each unit sold to the retailer, even with their name on it, and so we private labeled a shelving kit for the masses to be sold under the name of "(retailer)" to the end user consumer. Then they wanted to offer our full industrial products line to their own industrial customers, so we printed their name on the front of our cover and changed all photos so it speared with their name on the product. We called it the "Division "AA" Shelving Line" so it had a name but their logo and brand on it. (Many retailers do this now by creating in-house "brands" for sale in their own stores, or using "unique" model numbers for each retailer.) We agreed to take orders and ship in their name, direct to their customers, our entire product line. This meant we had to print multiple versions of our sales catalog with retail prices in it and create a discount schedule provided only to the retailer. The final customer would never know who we were; we would appear to be a division of the retailer shipping directly to them. We did this for several others, too, in the same formats.

Then we realized we could do this not just by private label but by distribution channel, so we printed catalogs with GOVERNMENT PROCUREMENT CONTRACT CATALOG, AUTOMOTIVE, and others. Their company or other contact number along with their contact information was specialty printed instead of ours. We suddenly did much more business because this was our early adaptation of a now common idea: shared marketing. It was especially practical for us since while the cover names and photos changed and the discount schedules might be different for each private label, our products never changed. They were always listed the same way in every catalog and only the names (and sometimes colors) changed. We ended up with over 20 different private label customers or categories, and sales exploded. We kept getting requests for more and thus we began to understand the power of private labeling. Their company name, address, phone and fax numbers were on the covers of our products. Orders rushed in from customers of various trades and industries, as well as governments both federal and local. All because we published private label catalogs.

REPRESENTATIVE REPRESENTATION

One top notch way to get new business is through the use of intermediaries. While they get a cut, you get more leads and more steered business. For non-retail businesses such as manufacturers and wholesalers, this occurs best through the use of non-employee but exclusive-to-your-product-line Manufacturers' Representatives ("Rep"). They are independent companies, persons, or contractors, who are not employees. They are paid by commission based on sales they bring to you or leads they provide that become orders. Typically, they are paid 30-60 days after you collect from your customer, but at least quarterly. These sellers have connections to many industries that they have developed over years and for many different product lines and services. They know that they must bring you orders to get paid, and so they have an incentive to ensure not only that you get orders, but that you are paid.

They know that for them to get paid you have to get paid, and the bigger the order, the more the commission. Think real estate sales. The Realtor gets you a buyer, and you in turn pay them a commission from the sales proceeds. No sale, no commission (unless you breach something). And no buyer, no sale. But they have exclusive and guaranteed commission rights, and that is part of the deal. When they cover you in a territory (geographical or business line) you agree to pay them whether someone in their territory is brought to you by them or just happens to call in. This requirement to pay regardless of how the customer comes to you is fair because your Rep can only represent you in the territory and no other direct competitor.

Many businesses on many industries pay by commission on sales, and the arrangement benefits both sides. So consider using a Manufacturers' Representative to help you get business if you are a manufacturer or wholesales.

And they do bring in business. In our shelving example, we used Reps. Almost half of our business eventually came in that way. While some customers did not know of or contact the Rep prior to buying, the Rep still got a commission because of the exclusive representation arrangement. It is fair to both sides, and it produces results for your business. Two pre-packaged promotional light duty steel shelving kits were developed for consumer sales. These were sold to retailers through Reps, until one titanic retailer wanted us to sell exclusively through them. We did, and made good profits from that channel for several years just from the one customer.

EXPANSION THROUGH EXPANSION

We tried out many other businesses, some of which did exceptionally well, and some of which did not do as well as we had hoped. A few just plain failed. The entrepreneur must accept that, like venture capitalists, not every investment or business idea will pan out. Nobody succeeds 100% of the time or makes a perfect deal 100% of the time. Even Warren Buffett claims to have missed on one or two investments. It happens. But the best way to succeed is to try.

So how best to grow your business? Well there are several ways, but the two best are through "greenfielding" and by acquisition.

Greenfielding is where you "sew the green fields and grow from scratch" and is a euphemism for growing through internal expansion. Let's use the analogy of a sports team. You can grow through draft picks or by trading for or signing someone as a free agent. Internal growth like draft picks is greenfielding. Acquisitions through trades or signings as free agents are equatable to the buying of a business and growing through acquisition. Either way works, but one or the other will be better for you due to your financial and structural condition.

Finances oftentimes dictate growth speed. If you lack the investment capital to grow, you can't grow very fast. And sometimes one or the other is cheaper. Sometimes it's cheaper to buy something, and other times it's cheaper to open a new store, warehouse, or plant. It all depends on the product or service, and your available capital.

The biggest warning is not to bite off more than you can chew. Overspend on an acquisition or expansion and it can make a successful business into an overstrained and teetering one. An example is Toys-R-Us. They were chugging along ok and then were taken private. While the Internet and Amazon and other competitors were making life hard for them, they could have survived. But the leveraged buyout saddled them with more than $5 Billion Dollars in debt, and their interest payments alone ate up all their operating profits. They collapsed under the weight of their own debt from the leveraged buyout. Had it never happened, they might still be selling toys in nearly a thousand stores. Now, they live on only in old commercials, the Internet, and in "pop-up" stores run by someone who bought the name in bankruptcy. 30,000 plus jobs are gone, and they bankrupted not just themselves but hundreds of large and small toymakers. Not how you want to expand.

There are several ways to grow. One is by buying at auction, another by finding a storefront or location that is overlooked or may be available because someone else failed and the rent may be lower just so the landlord can get someone into the space. Ask. You never know. And be prepared to jump right in. This requires you to have sufficient capital to do so. This means you must have a new or continuing original business plan that accounts for this.

You should be updating and rewriting your business plan yearly, if not twice a year. Constant recalculation of cash-flow, sales, profit, and future projections are critical not just to your expansion plans but to your survival as well. Make sure your Plan is always up-to-date and that you have adequate capital for expansion BEFORE YOU EXPAND.

And remember the investor's best friend: "buy low and sell high" and you'll always come out on top.

When we finally sold, it was another investor who benefited. They had the capital to buy us out and advance the business. (They dismantled the machines and shipped them overseas. Would you believe!)

Sometimes opportunity comes in an unusual way. We got into one business because of an accident. A company was selling machinery that was damaged by a tornado. I was offered it for basically the price of the cost of trucking because the seller had gotten an insurance settlement and needed to dispose of the machines. We bought them, shipped them into our facility, and then "repaired" them over the next six months. Most of them were restored to (if not perfect) operating condition, and we had a new product line because of an opportune buy. We could never have afforded them if they were new, but as salvage, they were a perfect and affordable deal.

In 1981 a reporter from the Philadelphia Bulletin business section wrote about me and my brothers, and how when other businesses were leaving our neighborhood we were not just surviving, but "As other firms abandon" the neighborhood "Steel Distributor expands and thrives." As many other industries closed or relocated, he wrote that my brothers and I stayed and expanded. I was quoted as saying "we're going against the trend on jobs and industries" as they left the City. "Hard times make companies tough; those surviving become better for the experience." We protected and even expanded our business, and we flourished. All because we had foresight, luck and a business plan.

We also invested in real estate. How that becomes your best investment will be addressed in Chapter 7.

CHAPTER SEVEN
The Real Estate Equation

Perhaps even above those of the stock market, returns on real estate investments are about the highest you can get for your investment where luck should not be a factor.

"Property is immutable." This is a maxim and a truism: there is only one of each unique piece of realty, and there will never be another like it. Each piece of land is unique even where there may be 1000 of the same house; no two pieces of land upon which they sit are the same. And that brings up the only most important rule of real estate: "Location, Location, Location." There is nothing that beats a building in the right place, whether it is because it so cheap you can buy it for nearly nothing and it is useful to you beyond the cost, or where it is pricey but situated in a place that will guarantee it will always have a ready set of buyers the moment it is put on the market. This is how housing stock in the United States and the rest of the world has been valued for centuries: build it in the right place and it will always sell. At a higher price than other equivalent-but-for-location properties.

People get rich from property. Just look at the Trump Empire, all built through real estate. In fact, many business people do the same thing but with a twist: your business rents its property, but from YOU. Huh?

Actually, a large number of businesses rent their facilities, and don't own them. Smart owners go one step further and create a company to own the underlying property. They make money both ways. Here's an example: McDonald's actually is made up of more than just McDonald's Corporation; in fact, there are two primary companies: one is the franchisor, the other is a real estate investment company named the Franchise Realty Corporation, created by Ray Kroc. A former McDonald's CFO once said that McDonald's wasn't really in the food business but was really in the real estate business and that the only reason they sold cheap burgers is because they generate revenue that the franchise tenants can use to pay McDonald's rent. McDonald's owns about half of the land and about 2/3 of the buildings that hold their franchisees, who pay McDonald's' real estate company rent. You can do this too.

The savvy investor, if they can afford it, buys the property in which their business will operate. They pay themselves rent. This has three advantages: they participate in any capital gains on the property, they cannot be evicted by a landlord or forced to leave due to rent increases, and they can use this method to take out money that a bank that has loans to the company would otherwise deny in dividends/distributions.

So how to do it? First, find a property. Then form an LLC or Subchapter-S Corporation to buy it. You own the underlying LLC or S-Corp. Then you can charge your business rent, and in many cases, this circumvents bank covenants against taking money out of the business by owners while the loans are still in force. As long as rent rates are reasonable for the market (don't overcharge) and the terms are similar to what you would encounter in an arms-length transaction with a non-affiliated landlord, you are going to be fine and pass muster. Also, you can get a mortgage for the property based solely on the anticipated rent stream, thus you can get a bank to help you buy it. After about 30 years it will depreciate to $0 but you will have gotten tax benefits each year that will lower taxes on the rent revenue and when it is sold it will likely sell for much more than you paid for it, assuming you sell. Once the mortgage is paid off you get all the revenue instead of some of it.

Wait... what about taxes, insurance, and maintenance? They are paid by the tenant: your business. This is called a "triple-net" lease and it is the most common among business leases. Few do not contain all three "nets" and so the landlord pays almost nothing except their mortgage (if they have one) and their own liability coverage. The tenant of a commercial (business) property pays real estate taxes, building and business insurance, and maintenance and repairs on the building as part of the lease. Even upgrades and modifications to the building are paid for by the tenant. This means that virtually all non-mortgage costs are borne by the tenant. This is why it is advantageous to own the property and collect rent "from yourself" if you possibly can.

But I saved the best part for last: bifurcation. Property owners who have a business in their building can many times bifurcate (partition or split) the building in such a way that more than just their business can be a tenant. So the business owner who also owns the building can make money from their business, rent from the business, and rent from other tenants. Think of the supermarket (or their owners) that owns the underlying shopping center property. They lease (sublease?) space to other businesses that do not compete like bookstores, shoe stores, banks, and restaurants. Thus, they are the anchor that draws customers, they make money from sales, and they make money from the leases; both theirs, and the other tenants of the shopping center.

You can do this too, with some foresight, a bit of luck, work to investigate properties, and some capital to buy the property. And actually, the best part is really that all of this is legal and common!

Back to our steel business. Real estate appealed to us because our initial strategy was buying and utilizing it for own company operations. We figured we could always sell it later for a profit. Things do affect real estate profits, both positively and negatively. While we had been brought up to believe that real estate was a good investment, it was still risky for us because we didn't have a lot of capital. Nonetheless, we thought it would be smart to own our own property. So, we decided we needed to draw up a Business Plan to analyze it in order to determine whether or not we would buy the underlying property and get into the real estate business along with the steel business.

We looked at buying real estate for two reasons. One, our small businesses were growing and we knew we would need more fabricating and storage space in the future. Two, we wanted to get the best return on our investments we could, and it seemed logical that buying and selling real estate, starting with the building we wanted to run our business from, was the best choice.

Neighborhoods change, for better or for worst. Some tenants don't pay rent on time, or even not at all. Some buildings are in decent shape and others look like a bomb went off inside. So we studied each neighborhood and region where we would be considering real estate for our business. We researched other properties in each area to get a feeling for the prices.

We even had concerns about nearby schools, housing, public transportation, retail stores and city government relations. And we decided that once we went into real estate we would go in whole hog and not just buy for our business, but also invest as a separate business in real estate both for commercial purposes, and in apartment houses and industrial buildings.

My other son John (the "not-the-co-author") is a Realtor. He deals with customers buying and selling real estate. While he has been very successful in it, he and I think differently about what makes people successful in business. He says you have to work "harder, not smarter" in what you do. I question that. Strange, but while we are not 100% in agreement, maybe both our views are right. He "sells" real estate, and he teaches real estate classes at a nearby university. He also gave motivational speeches. He used to be a reporter and publisher and has substantial experience in small business ownership and operation. He has worked for himself, and for others. (He prefers to be his own boss.) He became very successful as a Realtor and does well when he puts his effort into something.

I asked John "why work harder, not smarter" to succeed? His answer was short and to the point: make extra effort through hard work each day in every way. He does paperwork immediately after a client asks to make an offer, whether early in the day or late in the evening, instead of waiting until the end of the day or the next day as many other agents do. In one instance, he worked on paperwork until midnight to deliver a client's offer to the seller the next day. In order to make the sale he did the work. The offer, by the way, was accepted the next morning.

John is well prepared to provide for his clients' interests. He believes himself to be successful because he works harder on things like pre-approvals, pre-arranged times to meet clients, and getting a seller's permission to see a listing at a specific time. Presentations, negotiations, and offers to buy are done in proper sequence to make the sale. He makes sure he is always correct in what he does and is meticulous in his assurance that everything is done properly.

He's on the phone constantly, whether at home, on the street or in his office. He jokes about being on the phone at least 100 times a day. When we're together, he's on that phone over half the time, making or receiving a dozen calls in less than an hour. So, what he says is probably true. And his doing the hard work made him a success at what he does.

I'd say that working smarter is more important, yet John says he's more successful because he works harder than others in the same business. He gets cooperative referrals from competitors, leads from his own newspaper ads, and referrals from former clients. Sure, he probably works harder with longer hours, but one would think his closings are because he works smarter to get such results. So maybe both are true. Work harder and work smarter and no one can stop you!

I see John working harder… and smarter. To work smarter, you need a plan (a business roadmap) on how you can be more efficient in your business. John described his plan for finding prospective clients; bring sellers and buyers together, and how he'd close a sale.

In essence, you need a business plan to follow if you expect to be successful in selling and closing sales. That takes smarts, and hard work: following your plan is smart, and doing the things necessary to make it succeed involves hard work. My brothers and I used similar tactics when buying real estate years ago just like John today. John occasionally buys a property himself, and as any small business owner should do, he puts in gusto and hard work - and gets results.

- - - -

Buying real estate as a business is more than just getting a mortgage and repaying every month. It is maintenance and development and finding tenants and collecting rent; in short, it is a business like any other. Except it isn't like any other business. You first need to know what you can afford, and be prepared for problems. You also need to do more due diligence because you need to know what you don't know, like soil conditions and if there are any environmental or tax or lien issues lurking out there waiting to bite you in the you-know-where, hard.

Sometimes sellers (or governments) offer incentives to new property owners in blighted, dilapidated, or Enterprise-type zones. Rebates or discounts on taxes ("abatements"), labor incentives for tenants or owners who employ in the properties, potential and necessary repairs, and building codes and regulations all need to be identified before you buy. You have to have a good plan for real estate purchases just as for your new business. And you need skills that you may have to learn, or hire. Accounting, building management, sales (finding tenants), negotiation of terms and leases, attorneys (you will need protections in all agreements and help to draft the right ones), and maybe even rental agents and realtors early on, before you figure out how to do it yourself. And you need to know what you can get for rents and if they will be enough to cover your mortgages and other costs and generate a profit for you, or else why bother in the first place?!?

We had a "nose" for it, ourselves. That's how we succeeded in the first place. But to keep our success going, we had to refine our real estate procedures. We needed to know what to look for, where we should be looking, what we can afford or what we are willing to pay, and how we will manage each property. Your investment decisions should always be based on what you think the market will be in the future. Most of the time you can accurately project no more than one to three years hence. Most plans project for 5 or 10 years but are usually not accurate beyond three. Knowing what you can accomplish in those first three years will help you to figure out your prospects for the future. If you project a profit in three years, you likely will be successful. If not, quit before you lose your investment, and look elsewhere.

You can make a lot of money buying and selling commercial and industrial real estate. Here are some typical real estate deals we were involved in, over the years. First, I bought my own home. I borrowed the deposit money from my mother-in-law; she offered it to me and I accepted. The rest of the money came from a first mortgage from a bank. I would have a 30-year mortgage and expected my wages to provide the payment money each month. Just like most people.

When I sold it years later, after the mortgage was paid and my wife and I moved, the house sold for many multiples of what I had paid. (Today I understand it is worth several million dollars but I didn't get that much for it when I sold.) We did pretty well for ourselves while there, though. Over the years we hosted events where many famous people came to visit, party, or fundraise. We entertained Presidential candidates, Senators, Congressmen and women, Governors, Mayors, and a whole host of influential and famous people, including the likes of John Glenn, John Anderson, and Coretta Scott King (twice!). Our house was on the city House Tour for a number of years, and was famous and was listed in the National Historical Register because of the history and the architects who designed and built it in the 1860's.

And I learned that residential real estate was good for more than raising your family, too. You can get fantastic buys in residential real estate by leveraging the action. That means getting most of the money through mortgages or OPM ("Other People's Money"). I and my brothers entered the real estate market (mainly by accident) and became overnight successes in a new field. Sometime well after I bought my house my wife was walking and passed a beautiful double width, all brick apartment building, down the block from our house. She said to me "one day I'd like you to own a building like that!" Well, you know me. I called my brothers (we did everything together or not at all) and we looked it over. After some negotiating, we agreed to buy it. We didn't have a lot of cash since we'd sunk all our money into our manufacturing businesses, but we were able to scrape together just about enough to put the down payment in and buy the deal. Here is how it happened. I approached the woman who owned the building. It was run as a Christian Temperance rooming house, with nearly 2 dozen apartments; fifteen housekeeping and six were non-housekeeping. A former Governor of the state had owned it years earlier. We negotiated a price, put our down payment in, and mortgaged most of the rest. The owner lent us the balance in what is called "seller-financing" which is like mortgage but privately made by the owner and not a bank.

It took us months to clean out the liquor bottles and other trash and to repaint and fix up the property. Then, once it was presentable, we put up an "Apartments for Rent" sign with a price. They were small but cheap and clean. (It was more like a dormitory, and we eventually formed a company to own it and other properties that served as just that.) Within six months it was completely rented and making a profit before the end of the first year.

One times we sold a property for about double what we paid. Two men bought it from us and asked us to give them a seller finance for "fix-up money" so we did. We also registered our so-called seller mortgage and filed for liens against them and their wives, because they'd "joked" to me at settlement that "sometimes you don't get all the money on a sale once it's over." We thought about that and got worried, so we recorded the liens. Two years later, they defaulted. They claimed the heating system was bad and they needed our money to replace it. That was a con story, and we saw right through it. We exercised the lien two weeks later and we got our money in full from them. The morale of that story: "No deal is final until it is paid for in full."

Another deal came from former bank president who I became friendly with because we both served on a charity board together. He had an "in" to buy a 100-unit apartment house but didn't have the money. Having lost everything in his recent divorce, he was remarried and cash strapped.

His bank was being taken over and he was losing his job. But he had a way to buy this property cheap and others didn't. Interesting where opportunities come from. My brothers and I agreed to supply the down payment funds and partner with him 50/50 on ownership, subject to certain stipulations by us. We needed the depreciation and he needed the income, so we split that way: 50/50 on the profits, 95% of the depreciation to us. Unbeknown to us, prior to our funding the down payment, he had pledged 10% of the deal to someone else. Since he told us afterwards, it was required of him that the 10% was to come out of his end of the deal.

To get operating money for the building we went to the current owner, and after hard, long negotiating sessions, he agreed to give us seller financing of 10% of the price for market interest rates, for 5 years. This would work because he would the rest of the money at settlement. Our partner got us a mortgage that included extra funds to upgrade the property so a contractor could be hired to make repairs. New storm windows, a new roof, insulation, some upgraded kitchens, and a new guard to replace the doorman were all part of the renovations. A newfangled computer-controlled system was to be installed to turn heat on and off at certain times. Our partner arranged for electric meters for each apartment and even got a rebate on the cost from the contractor after the job was completed. All from an accident and a friendship.

We started our first year with a surplus of money, and the upkeep costs were low (but so were rents). At least tenants now paid their own electric charges. What we did was use the upgrades to justify raising rents by 20% the next year, but were still at half of what other buildings got. So we were full but revenues were far below what they could be. As tenants left, we replaced them with higher paying ones, and things were going well. Then a big piece of bad luck intervened. Our partner was biking and fell and cracked his head open. He also got served with divorce papers from his new (2d) wife that same week. Up to then he had been doing the books for the building. He also, we found out, owned another smaller apartment building in a dingier section of the city, where one of his tenants fell down the elevator shaft and suffered major injuries. Sadder still? Our partner had no insurance coverage for that property to cover the accident. This all happened in the space of one week. My brothers and I thought that this was a bit too much risk and we decided we needed to end the partnership. We offered to buy out our partner for a large equitable sum and he turned around and offered us the same plus 10% more to buy us out. It was ethical that if we could buy him out, he could buy us out. We accepted. Later on, we found out that he didn't have other investors like we thought, but that he had an arrangement to sell it for a ludicrous profit. But we chose our exit and made our profit and we got our end of the deal and he got his. Everyone was happy except me - I wanted to buy him out; but we sold instead. We should have gotten more money on our end, but we did the right and ethical thing. And that's another lesson: be ethical and be fair, and others will tend to do the same. It's all about reputation, and yours is enhanced every time you keep your word.

SUCCESS REQUIRES 100% OVERSIGHT

Small Business owners have to pay attention to their business operations at all times. They may have to pay even more attention when they think they know all the details that make their business successful, but really don't. This is especially true in real estate.

Any one of a hundred little things can ruin you if you don't pay attention to every detail. Owning a property is like owning your house, but in multiples. Not only do you have to pay your mortgage and bills monthly, but you have to collect rent, maintain the property, deal with and repair any problems and troubles, and make sure you are always overseeing it.

The old adage is that your home is the largest investment you will ever make.

Wrong.

Your business is the largest investment you will ever make. And you have fewer protections than with your home. Residences have a myriad of laws to help homeowners stay in their homes if they suddenly lose their jobs and cannot pay. Foreclosure is more difficult, and tenants have more protections than landlords. The law protects homeowners from tax liens and other seizure-methods during the winter, and provides substantial due process for homeowners to prevent their homes from being seized out from under them.

Businesses have no such protections and commercial properties lack them, too. Your business is subject to seizure by the government, tax authorities, and creditors through the courts. They can sue you, and place liens against you for almost any legitimate reason. You have few if any protections since you most likely have signed personally for the business bank loans as a condition of the loans. You can lose your house, savings, and pension if you default on a business loan, whereas you cannot lose these things in most other cases. Insurance will only help if you have enough - and you are not blocked from coverage by restrictions policy limits that apply to businesses but not consumers.

Real estate has special risks. The biggest is that you are spending substantially more on your purchase and operations that on your home, and your monthly payments are going to be much bigger as a result. Most businesses do not get the luxury of 30-year mortgages but rather 10 year or 15 year with payments amortized as if they were 30 years – with a balloon payment of anywhere from 65-80 percent of the loan due at the end of the term, which are usually refinanced again and again. (Most 30-year mortgages work such that you are not paying more of the payment in principal than interest until about the 23rd year, meaning that it takes about 23 out of 30 years until half of the principal of the loan is paid; the rest is interest.) Your interest rates for business loans and commercial mortgages are also higher, and they adjust with the market. Typically, they are some amount of percent above the "Prime Rate" which is the rate the largest and most creditworthy businesses pay. This means that if your home mortgage is 4%, your business mortgage is probably 6% and will change up or down the moment interest rates change. And they go down less than they go up, and they usually have a "floor" or interest rate below which they will not drop, such as in this example, probably is 5%. Commercial mortgages are also more easily callable and foreclosable, and lenders usually require you to have your business bank account in their bank and this allows them the ability to "set-off" against your account. A set-off is where a bank can take funds from one account to pay a deficit in another; they can take the money from your checking account and put it toward a past due business loan payment. Most loans have set-off agreements in them and require you to keep your business savings and checking accounts in their bank so that they can specifically have set-off rights against them. Another risk. Don't let this happen.

The conclusion? Small businesses owners must have a "hands on" approach at all times for their business to be successful and profitable, and to prevent trouble and loss. Real estate provides better returns and can yield gargantuan profits over time. But they also require more time and effort to oversee and must be constantly watched and evaluated.

There is one other issue with real estate that makes it different: it is possible (and it happened to us) to buy a property without even realizing you've made an offer on it. How?

I and our Realtor were driving past a property we had recently purchased using his help. At one point he chimed in "How would you like to buy a multi-million-dollar building, at a fraction of the price? My mother-in-law inherited it from her late husband. Interested?"

No. I didn't like the location. I told him so as we drove past it. It was in the wrong part of town. If it was closer to the center of the city, maybe I'd give him the price. He persisted. "Just drive past and look at it." So to shut him up we drove there and inspected it. In jest, I made him an offer of one one-hundredth of what they were asking; I was sure his client would refuse it and that way, he'd stop pressuring me to buy it, or the client would counter offer and I could refuse.

The next day he called me, and my bluff. His mother-in-law accepted my ridiculous lowball offer. I was shocked, but very thankful. Fortunately, we'd gotten a real deal on this property only because the price was so ludicrously lower than what it was worth (I understand the current owner listed it recently for about $5 million dollars. Wish we'd have gotten that!) So what would've happened if I'd said "it was a joke offer" to his acceptance? I'd probably have been sued. At settlement, we finally bought the building for less than 10% of the original listing price, just a few thousand dollars. We sold it years later for substantially more, to the then-tenant. And we made a nice profit. (But not millions.)

The moral is to never make an offer in jest; it could lead to a valid acceptance at your own peril.

But there is another moral; and it is one I learned from my father: You make your money on the BUY, not the SELL. If you buy it cheap enough, it doesn't really matter how much you sell it for.

For nearly a decade I served as President of an Enterprise Zone in Philadelphia. I learned about financial incentives for locating in Zones. We even bought a property in a Zone for our real estate investment portfolio, and made a profit on it when it was sold some years later. While there were both good and bad tenants (some are trouble free profit machines and others cost you time, money, and some of your hair) overall it was profitable. And property can bring other financial benefits beyond tenants.

We bought this Zone building at a time when cellphones were in their infancy. There were three large phone antenna discs on the roof. They became our property at when we bought the building, along with the $20,000 per year income per disk. This helped cover overhead costs on the building. It turned out that cellphone companies, in those early days, needed rooftops to put their antennas on. So did cable companies. We rented out the roof and made almost as much money from the towers and disks as we did from the tenants below them. When you buy a property, with rare exceptions, you buy the sky above it and the land below it as well. Air rights and ground rights can produce income and profits through rental, mining, and space for storage. Imagine you have a 10-story office building with 3 floors of parking and 6 floors of offices, plus the lobby floor. You can rent the parking at night to residents of nearby apartments, in addition to providing parking for daytime tenants. You also get rental from tenants, and you can rent out space on the roof for antennas, ad billboards, and other things we haven't thought of yet. Profits breed invention.

You have to be a visionary to see opportunities coming from the startup of a small business. Real estate is no exception. Sometimes, you can't see the forest for the trees, but you can see the trees. Maybe what is needed is a ladder so you can go above and see the forest. Property is immutable. It is as permanent as anything on this Earth. And if it has the right (or a good enough) location, location, location, it can be immensely profitable either from the rental of it or the ownership and sale of it. From buying one apartment for rent to a family or relocated worker, to a mammoth building with 500 units in it, the potential is there. And while scale brings better returns, you can do well on one if you plan it out right, execute against that plan and do not deviate, and get busy working to make it happen. And, of course, luck never hurts.

Chapter 8 brings information on how to finance your enterprise. Check it out!

CHAPTER EIGHT
Sources of Funds and Financing for New Businesses

Everyone knows what an elevator is. It takes people up, and down, and does all of it in just a few minutes. In fact, the average elevator ride is under 90 seconds. In a claustrophobic, sealed-in environment with no escape until the elevator doors open on a floor.

The "Elevator Pitch" is taken from that. It is a sales pitch that is timed to be delivered in the amount of time you have the "target" of your pitch "cornered" so to speak. Imagine getting into an elevator alone with Warren Buffett or Bill Gates (or even Elon Musk) and having just the amount of time of that elevator ride to pitch your new business idea to them in the hopes they'll like it and agree to invest in it. That pitch must be concise, on point, and give enough information about your concept or idea to convince an investor to want to hear more.

Think of the movie "Working Girl" where Melanie Griffith's character gets just one minute, in an elevator, to convince Philip Bosco's character that she, and not someone else, came up with a particular business idea that he is about to spend millions on, or not. She does so, and convinces him it was really her idea, not her ex-boss's. And it's a good idea, too. And he believes her because she made it convincing, factual, and showed how it benefited him; and told the simple truth, not an elaborate embellishment. With backing documents and facts.

You need to prepare to do the same. Now it is ridiculous to think you will actually be delivering this speech in the setting of an elevator, but one never knows. The point of it is that you need a quick, precise, convincing argument to convince a potential investor (or employee or partner) to want to hear more. And given the short attention spans in today's world, you probably don't have more than a minute or two to deliver it. Thus, the Elevator Pitch concept: 90 seconds to fame and fortune, or failure and financial ruin. "Shark Tank" but for real.

This book is not about elevator pitches, but I can give you a few pointers on how to craft an elevator pitch. Here's the "elevator pitch" on elevator pitches:

Tell your "target" who you are, what your idea is, what you intend to do, how it will be successful, and why he/she should invest. Hone it to 50 or so words so it can be tailored to a 40-45 second pitch, and be prepared to answer these questions in the remaining 30-45 seconds: how will the investor be repaid a profit, and why they should invest, they are being asked, and they stand to gain. Always maintain eye contact, and always be prepared to show why you came to them and not someone else. This is about convincing someone in less than a minute that they are special and they are the one to invest in your business. They don't want to hear how (or that) you asked 37 people before them (but they might ask who anyway). They want to believe you only asked them, not anyone else, or asked them first. And that there's a reason you asked them besides that they have money. Perhaps your pitch includes how you hope to gain from their expertise, mentoring, or connections in a way other investors can't provide. On the flip side, you need to impress them with your character, demeanor, poise, preparation, and choice of them and not someone else. Have a "hook" and an exit strategy for them. Show them, in less time than it takes to make toast, how you have invented a better toaster and why they are the one to benefit from investing in it, and how it will enrich them both more and faster than something else. And prove it's viable.

In less than 90 seconds.

Less than 60 seconds is better.

If I read the paragraph above out loud, it would take about 90 seconds. Be faster, tighter, and better. This book is about giving you the tools, so it elaborates. In an elevator pitch, which is basically a chance to take a literal minute of someone's highly valuable time, you have less time for prose and must make every $ingle word count. Profitably. (☺)

- - - -

Financing comes in all forms, from the unconventional to the conventional, especially in this new era of money sourcing from more than just banks and rich investors. Now with venture capital funds and crowdfunding there are more ways than ever to seek funding for your new idea. But that doesn't mean someone will necessarily fund it. It still has to show how it will make the investor richer or otherwise meet or satisfy a goal of the investor. As for me, the past owner of a conglomerate of small businesses, I learned early on to constantly seek dependable, long-term money sources. No matter where they might come from.

Whether you invest in a startup, purchase part of the whole of an existing business, or invest with a group in businesses such as retailers, manufacturers, or real estate, knowing what financial sources are available invariably makes the difference between success and failure.

You need good sources of capital to give small businesses their on-going and additional funds when needed, whether to cover overhead costs, additional working capital or even to rehabilitate parts of a small business (or liquidate part or all of it). Seeking sources of funding from traditional sources like banks and investors, as well as non-traditional sources like crowdfunding or venture capitalists, is the lifeblood for small business people who want to grow or to build a business.

A retired small businessman I knew told me "the biggest problem for small business has got to be undercapitalization. The joy of owning and running your own business quickly becomes overshadowed by the reality of having to pay bills. Maybe the most important aspect of your business continuing is your cash-flow. Money in, money out! That's what it's all about."

His receivables were the lifeblood of his business, helped by advantageous credit terms and discounts. The ability to pay vendors, rent, electricity and your own salary gives you freedom to concentrate on growing your core business. Of course, you can cut some expenses by working from home, which is very common for new small businesses. But not all startups lend themselves to it. Some can get by through using shared spaces, others require private offices. Some need facilities and/or storefronts, which preclude working from home.

One rule of thumb someone taught me always stuck with me. It made sense and was quite poignant. Warehouse your product at your supplier. "If your business requires inventory, use your vendor's warehouse when possible. Tight inventory controls and counts are important. High inventory takes money out of your pocket and sits there in inventory. If it doesn't get used, it's the same as burning money," my friend said. He was right! Thanks buddy.

Small businesses need what is often considered "creative" financing; here are some ideas.

First and foremost are your own savings or that of family members. Note that loans from family create schisms that oftentimes cannot be repaired if the money is lost because the business fails, and borrowing from friends is the surest-fire way to lose your friends. Even for a "sure thing" investment. Something always goes wrong. And at the worst time. But still, these sources are the first you should seek.

Next come your other investment generating assets: credit cards. Many first-time small business owners start by financing their business using their credit cards. If they can expect to pay the bills off and not get into default, it is a good way to finance your startup, and many cards give you points or miles or cash when you use them. Beware two catches, though: almost all consumer credit cards have terms that forbid use for business purposes and can be canceled if you are found to do so, and if the business can't pay at least the minimum payment each month, you are personally responsible since the credit line is in your name. Your credit is the one that will be ruined, and you may have to declare bankruptcy personally, not the business. You can lose your credit, your home, and your new business this way. And while we're on the subject, the one absolute no-no is to never take out a second mortgage or HELOC loan against you home if you can't be sure you can pay it off if the business fails, or you will lose your home. No kidding. Banks couldn't care less. They just want their money. On Time.

Obtaining sufficient financing continues to be a major concern for all small businesses. But if you need funds and don't have enough yourself or through your close family and friends, it's time to visit your friendly neighborhood bank loan officer. (Hint: they're not so friendly unless you can prove you can repay your loan.) They will all want some form of collateral, including liens on receivables, equipment, property or leases, and will want you, as owner, to sign personally making you personally liable and on the hook for the money if the business fails. See, you can still lose your house and ruin your credit. Fun, huh?

Banks aren't the only source. Venture capitalists and individual investors also invest in startups, but only if they stand to make large multiples of their investment back and usually within 3-5 years. All will require you to have for them an "exit strategy" of either being profitable enough to buy them out at a huge profit, or a public stock sale (more on this later) or private sale to another company or investor. And the profits aren't 5%-

10% per year but 300%-500% over 3-5 years. Some will go out as far as 7 years but most "angel investors" as they are called want out in less than 5 years and they want 3-5 times their money. This usually equates to a 25%-50% per year increase in their ownership valuation each year. If you can't show how this will happen and how they will exit, it's unlikely they will invest. Remember this for your elevator pitch.

Of course, you can go to what is called the "capital markets" – a fancy term for the stock market. But few companies can meet the requirements of scale and critical mass (size) required. And most companies must be able to "float" (issue) no more than a third of their authorized stock shares and have that valuation be at least $25 million or so to qualify. And most brokers who underwrite your offering (guarantee to support it and make sure the shares actually get sold during the opening day of trading in your stock in the initial public offering or "IPO") won't underwrite anything where less than 10 million shares are issued because nearly 2/3 of all stock shares are sold to or by (and owned by) hedge and other funds ("institutional investors") and not individuals like you and me. Institutions are usually giant pension funds like Oppenheimer or Fidelity or T. Rowe Price or the State of California. They trade 10,000 or 100,000 shares at a time to generate scale and see profits from small movements in price. So if you can't float at least 10 million shares (for at least $10 or so per share) in your new offering you probably can't go public. Then there's the little matter of having to be (or convert to) a C-Corp. Only a C-Corporation can issue stock publicly through the U.S. stock markets by law except for real estate investment trust(s) ("REIT") which are partnerships that must distribute 95% of their profits annually to investors.

And going public isn't cheap. It can literally cost millions to do this so you better be able to raise a lot! (Underwriting costs get paid up front.)

So what if you can't issue stock publicly? You can do it privately, in private placements or through limited offerings. Each has rules and not only must you meet the federal rules but each state has stock investment rules you must adhere to. These are so-called "blue-sky" laws and each state has a different one. Also, to sell private stock or investment shares to investors through private placements or a private offering prospectus, each investor must be income and asset "qualified" according to federal regulations. And it costs lots to make a prospectus.

OK. So what do you do if you can't get any of these or if you have gotten as much as you can but need more financial help for your fledgling startup?

One bright opportunity for attractive financing can be had in special opportunity sectors called (city and state) Industrial Opportunity Zones, as well as federal Enterprise Zones. There are also similar programs covering buildings located in older, blighted industrial areas. While the shopping list of problems in those areas are legend due to unemployment and crime, and some areas are rundown and contain older, multi-story buildings, that's not all. Infrastructure is also poorly maintained in these areas. For example, many narrower streets have potholes or trash strewn about. Local and state governments encourage new private and public investments in these zones (and elsewhere) and offer incentives to businesses locating there are bringing new jobs. These incentives include tax-exempt bonds, tax abatements and TIF credits (we discussed this earlier), job tax credits and/or job training reimbursements, mortgage guarantees, equity loans, and low interest financing. Some even have both worker-training grants and programs to train workers that have no cost to the new business, and some provide grant money for new businesses. All of this is done for two reasons: Redevelopment, and JOBS. These types of creative financing come in many packages in conjunction with federal SBA programs, as well as "Fame" and other local and regional economic development corporations, and even local banks. Some banks are required to reinvest in their communities as conditions of their banking licenses and so they offer lower interest loans and other breaks to new businesses, especially minority and women owned ones (who have traditionally had a much harder time starting up and getting business).

All of that is added to the additional incentives that many utilities provide: discounts, set-up costs, location information, and assistance with establishing your business and merging into the community where you will locate.

Such inducements bring economic development to depressed, blighted or highly unemployed areas. They bring in businesses that they hope will stabilize neighborhoods, improve housing stock and quality, and bring up neighborhood values. Most importantly, new businesses bring added tax revenue bases for the city, from wage taxes, income taxes, and real estate taxes, many of which also are granted discounts or abatements for some period of time as incentives in certain neighborhoods or for creating certain types of higher-paying jobs.

All this vitalization means new jobs and a resurgence of optimism for distressed areas. And it also means new and inventive ways for you to get financial assistance for your new business if you are willing to open in one of these Zones.

Small businessmen and women need seed money, bank lines of credit, and working capital to make their business survive. Many municipal downtown shopping streets contain businesses like laundromats, printers, bookstores, retailers, beauty shops, and restaurants. Add to this the workshops and Zone businesses in the wholesaling and manufacturing trades and they have a secure tax base. This funds schools, services like police and fire, and other services for residents and businesses alike. Any business that can promise jobs and tax revenue that appears stable will get the most bang for their sought-after buck from these government programs designed to help ensure that the new business succeeds and hires and pays taxes and thrives.

When jobs are created, state welfare and unemployment payments are reduced; neighborhood residents take pride in their homes and improve the physical appearance of their community. With new businesses joining in, the added city and state revenues can pay back the costs of the many financial incentives needed to bring in these businesses through the use of incentives. And once an area appears to "turn around" and redevelop, it encourages even more capital investments and this vicious cycle is actually beneficial to all: the municipality gets more tax revenue and private redevelopment of blighted areas; the residents get more options and a cleaner, safer area to travel to and fro in; the businesses get more new businesses to buy from and sell to.

Everybody Wins.

- - - -

The first year or two for most new business ventures are generally non-profitable or barely so. Since many businesses can usually get tax credits, tax benefits, and low interest rate loans for investing in certain areas, new businesses have much to gain with these and other forms of creative financing. It is a great option for small businesses to consider.

What about that traditional financing? Banks want proof you will succeed; really, proof you will be able to pay back the loan plus the interest. New businesses quickly tap out their bank lines and their credit cards, if any. New cash for expansion, operations, or just to enhance cash-flow comes from new partners and other investors. But some don't have a choice; to survive they may need new money that only comes from a sale or control or even all of the company. Failing to raise sufficient money to run the company invariably leads to a forced sale, bankruptcy, or even closing the business. None of these are acceptable to the true entrepreneur.

Three other important ways to get new cash are through leverage: factoring your receivables, getting suppliers to extend payment terms, and getting customers (when not paying on receipt) to pay quicker. Generally, when a business makes a good profit but a majority of customers take longer to pay than the terms offered to them, a business finds itself in a cash bind, unable to pay bills owed to suppliers of services or merchandise or employees' wages. To solve this, businesses often offer discounts for faster pay such as "2% 10, Net 30." This means that if a customer pays by the 10th day after receipt of the goods, they can take a 2% discount. Otherwise, they pay full price by 30 days. This is a standard discount payment formula for manufacturers to extend to customers. Sometimes taking a credit card costs 2%-3% but means nearly instantaneous payment and cash now instead of a month or two later. Saves on billing and deposit costs, too. Others, particularly in retail, use "Factors." A Factor is a company, an intermediary agent really, that finances your receivables (the money owed to you by customers). They pay you right away for each invoice you issued and they collect it on the usual terms from the customer. They discount the payment to you by a few percent so you get less but get it now. No collection costs and less accounting and paper work. The Factor charges a commission and fees in the form of the discount. This is common in large retail and particularly so for department stores. "DP's Stores" buys clothing lines from "YourCo." YourCo wants to be paid immediately but DP's doesn't have the cash until they sell some of the goods. So you factor the invoices. FactorCo buys the invoices from you and you assign them to FactorCo. They pay you $.97 cents on the dollar (a 3% discount, if you will) and you get you money the next day. FactorCo collects the whole invoice amount from DP's 60 days later, just as the terms require. You get paid now but at a discount, and FactorCo makes a profit. DP's is happy because they can offer the goods for sale for two months before they have to pay. Everyone wins.

Other tricks for better cash-flow include deposits and prepayments. On large and on custom orders, ask for a deposit of, say, 25% or 50%. In advance. Most customers will pay it if they want the goods, especially with custom or private-label goods. Next, review how your customers have paid their bills in the past. Do any take allowances (credits for mistakes, bad product, etc.)? Regularly? Is it always the same customers? (If so, maybe they should pay higher prices or have limits on returns.) Does a small group of the same customers always pay late? Do they argue about late fees and interest charges or just pay them? Late interest charges should be strongly enforced, when necessary.

We once had a customer who always took an allowance for about 10% of the order every single time. We figured out, with some insight from friendly competitors, that they did this to stall paying the bill while the allowance process worked its way through each time. We solved this by first raising the price by 5% just for them, and then lowering it by 5% but not permitting allowances unless claimed immediately upon arrival without a corresponding delay in payment, and finally, we just came to the conclusion that they weren't worth the trouble and we dropped them as a customer. Not the preferable solution but we were spending most of the profits on their orders dealing with the allowance claims and waiting to be paid. In the end, you need to make hard decisions; one of them is knowing when to "fire your customer."

Late paying and constantly complaining customers need to be closely monitored. More problematic customers should be put on a cash-only basis. Cash or Check on Delivery terms should always be offered before orders are picked up or shipped. It can't hurt to ask. Payment terms to all regular customers should be short and beneficial to you: "1% - 5 Days, Net 15" for example, instead of "Net 30" days. Or just require payment on delivery or pickup. Customers understand you're running a business, not a charity. While they fight for every discount and advantage they can get, they do with their customers what you are proposing for them. As I said, it can't hurt to ask. The worst that can happen is they say "no" and revert to the usual terms. Ask for payment up front or at shipment. Offer discounts for fast pay; many will avail themselves of it and while you get a bit less, the benefits are fast cash-flow turnaround and lower or eliminated billing and collection costs.

(I realize many of these suggestions work better for manufacturing or other industrial businesses and not so much for retail. Adjust as best you can and use what works for you.)

Invoices on shipped goods should be dated the same day the shipment is made; preferably mailed or transmitted to the customer that very same day. If you ship at 4:59 PM, send the invoice by 6:00 PM that day.

To get your money faster, allowances can be offered to settle past due disputed outstanding receivables, including accounts in litigation. Even though costly to do so, cash will be available to help solve any immediate cash shortage. DO THIS ONLY AS A LAST RESORT.

On the accounts payable side, slow moving inventories should be closed out and not replaced. On purchased goods or services, suppliers should be asked to temporarily extend longer terms to pay your bills. If 60 days solves most cash-flow problems, regular supplier sources will probably do it, although they might charge you a few percent more for some goods. Better is to ask to make payments on one-third of the total amount of each bill to be paid on a 30, 60- and 90-day terms payment basis. Get creative, and work both ends to get faster pay from your customers while getting more time to pay your own bills.

Actually, the best thing is to get your suppliers to "consign" or "warehouse" merchandise. This is where you don't pay for goods until 15-30 days after they're actually sold to your customer. Some suppliers are overstocked themselves and may offer to do this to get unwanted inventory off their own floor and onto yours. Auto dealers, large retailers ordering seasonal Holiday merchandise, and marketers of seasonal Holiday sales do this all the time. You become a consignment shop, and collect sales revenue before paying for the goods yourself. Not a bad idea.

Plan NOW for better cash-flow management, especially in today's economy. Opportunities to grow and prosper are a challenge for all of us. Believe me it's true: CASH IS ALWAYS KING. [*Credit is Queen?*]

- - - -

Today's businesses are in a period of rapid change. But that's no different from any other era. Interest rates rise, right now from historic lows, but they rise and fall. Prospects for the near term could be flat or optimistic; future market demand could weaken due to inflation, energy and interest costs, or political events. You may encounter (or need) downsizing, weakened sales... and lower profits. This will make loans harder, not easier, to obtain. All in continuous cycles.

These changes oftentimes result in job loss, sales declines, and less service and less money in the marketplace. Ensuring your business has sufficient financing is a never-ending concern. So use all of the resources at your command. Bargain with sellers, plead with buyers, negotiate with governments, and use every advantage you can get. Your business creates jobs. Jobs reduce welfare and unemployment payments. Businesses increase tax and fee collections for governments. These added revenues pay back the costs of many government financial incentives many times over, but more than that; governments exist to serve their citizenry. The best way they do this is with job creation so that all taxpayers can comfortably afford to be just that – taxpayers. They provide infrastructure so that businesses can create jobs in this continuing cycle of employment, taxes, and new businesses. So towns and states see this kind of incentive granting as a form of investment in the future of their region, and how it helps to fulfill their purpose as government of the people and for the people.

HOW TO ENSURE YOUR FINANCIAL STABILITY; MANAGENT OBJECTIVES

Every business has to have good record keeping habits. Without them, meeting tax and bank accounting and payment requirements fails. You will be creating a budget to figure how to price your products or services, and to determine if your prospective venture is financially feasible. You will have to file forms and get permits and licenses. You will need to hire, so you will need job applications. (Even if you do this online, you will need paper somewhere for government reporting.) Timecards, performance reviews, production and sales reports, all must be designed and created. Remember the Business Plan from Chapter 4?

Projected income statements, balance sheets and cash-flow statements are needed. Startups must research to find facts or data that helps to improve these estimates. A good accountant cannot only do these things for you, but can keep you out of trouble. Ditto for a good attorney. Bigger companies usually have their own bookkeeper and controller (the smaller company version of the CFO) who keep the books, process payroll, collect and disburse funds, and make sure your cash-flow is always positive. (Otherwise you're in trouble.)

Here are some important questions that need to be answered before you open your business:

1. How much will it cost to start this business?

2. What will be my weekly/monthly/annual expenses?

3. What's it cost to buy/produce/deliver my products/services?

4. Where can I get all this information before I open my doors?

5. What services can I expect from my accounting firm and from my law firm? Do I need them? [*Yes! Yes! Yes!*]

6. Where will I get the money to start and sustain my business?

7. What will I have to offer as collateral on a loan? Do I have it?

8. What do lenders consider for loans to small businesses?
   Can I meet the requirements?

9. Am I eligible for government loans or grants?
   How do I get them if I do?

10. How strong is my personal credit? What's the risk to it if I fail?

11. Who do I know who might invest in or finance my business?
    How can I convince them to invest?

12. What permits/licenses/certifications do I need?
    How do I get them?

13. What did I forget in this list? Can I succeed if I forget them?

Let's figure where funds can come from by capital via the Capital Equity route

1. Tap Your Personal Money Tree For Funds. For your start-up in a small business, how about a friendly source? Ask relatives, friends, and immediate family members to invest.

2. Personal Loans. These come from individuals, and not banks or funds.

3. Personal Savings. It is recommended that you put money in a savings or checking account at the bank you will use before you borrow from that bank. You can even take out a small personal loan, even if you don't need the money right away, to establish creditworthiness. Note that most banks will require this if they lend to your business if the company is small and you are the only, or primary, owner.

4. Look For Investors. Unrelated venture capital funders might be willing to invest in your business as limited or silent partners. As you grow or start a new venture more investors can come in. Your company's ideas and potential growth could even spark a future public offering. Just be aware that these investors want quick and substantial results.

5. Home Loans. This is DANGEROUS. Do this only as a last resort. A new mortgage, or a re-mortgage, or a home equity loan (HELOC) can provide funding. However, this risks losing the property, which is usually your home. You must own it and have sufficient equity and income to qualify.

6. Credit Cards. Credit cards can help you obtain cash in advance or for general spending. Many entrepreneurs take out cash advances on their cards. But the interest rates are high (3-5 times what you'd pay with a conventional loan) and come with high fees. They must be paid back on time or you're going to be forced into personal bankruptcy. VISA, MasterCard, Discover and American Express all provide these advances. Be forewarned: most cardmember agreements specifically and strictly prohibit the use of personal cards for business spending. So use care in doing it, and be discreet.

7. Cashing in Insurance Policies, Stocks, Bonds, Retirement and Profit-Sharing Accounts, and CD's. These are all possibilities of last resort. Each has a penalty attached; and while you can liquidate or borrow against some of these instruments, you do so with either tax or cash penalty consequences and you lose their availability if you fail and don't restore them. Selling your future inheritances or insurance policies in viatical deals can be costly to do (because payments are discounted far beyond their net present value) and may not be legal in all jurisdictions. Do not take this step without consulting both an accountant AND an attorney. And never do it in haste. (Preferably not at all.)

Investment Capital through OPM (Other Peoples' Money)

1. Types of Loans. Banks and mortgage brokers need to be shopped like a suit of clothes. Be careful, bankers are NOT your partners. Anything but! Bank loans are generally given to businesses against the accounts' receivables, with factoring or lock-box service (where payments are sent to the bank's post office box and deposited into the loan account; excesses are deposited into the company checking account) generally required or longer-term loans.

2. Partners. Especially in real estate and retail marketing deals, bring people or companies together who want to make money. Take in a partner who has the cash in exchange for your work and experience.

3. Trade Credit. Many suppliers will provide you open account payment terms for 30 to 90 day waits until you must pay in full. It's like an American Express credit card but with longer terms, but where you must still pay in full when the bill finally comes due. This "dating" time from suppliers means extended time to pay bills to them for materials or merchandise you sell.

4. Leasing. Leasing cars, merchandise and equipment doesn't affect your line of credit, but the tradeoff is that you don't own the underlying asset. However, in exchange, you can upgrade more often, and write off 100% of the leasing costs for business used items on your business taxes each year. This conserves capital and provides a tax benefit.

160

5. Consigned Stock. You get inventory to sell and pay for it when it does. That's how many gift shops, used clothing stores, used home furniture stores and even new and used automobile dealers work. They stock cars on their lots on consignment, only paying the manufacturer for them once they are sold. Sellers keep a commission or percentage of the sale and send the "base price" back to the consignor.

6. Public and Government Loan Sources. They may be available for low cost fix-up building loans, or for a loan to buy the entire building. The SBA guarantees certain qualifying bank loans for commercial borrowers from banks. Industrial Development Corporations ("IDC's") provide select loans at below "prime" interest rates to small businesses that are relocating to a specific area the IDC wants to promote. Cities and states may have set-asides for micro- and small- businesses through various Community Development Organizations that help get your business financing sources; some even have the ability to loan directly to certain qualifying businesses.

7. Participation with Larger Companies. Labor-intensive jobs and smaller product fabrications are cheaper and more efficient when you partner with a larger company and have them private label, for you! Many have special deals for first-time small business customers.

RESOURCES FOR ASSISTANCE TO NEW SMALL BUSINESSES

There are a bunch of organizations, professionals, and agencies that provide advice and even financial and other resources to new businesses. Some exist solely for that purpose. SCORE and the Small Business Administration ("SBA") are two of them. Other resources than these include:

1. Lawyers and Accountants, who can answer legal and accounting information.

2. The Department of Commerce (city, county, region) can get business leads for you. So can the Better Business Bureau if your new locale has one. Join them and use them!

3. Trade, business and civic organizations are ideal for market information, who to contact for buying, selling or swapping business merchandise and ideas with other firms.

4. Suppliers can help you with information you are looking for to sell their products or how to value-add (manufacture something using their product into a new one) their goods.

5. Consultants (like non-competitors and competing companies located outside of your market area) can help you with advice and ideas (as long as they don't feel threatened).

6. Insurance and Business Brokers give service and ideas, and provide products that can help to both run and protect your business.

7. College and University Business schools can work with you on projects utilizing their graduate students for research on how to sell to a specific trade or to work part time for you or volunteer on projects of your small business. These students sometimes work as interns in exchange for college credit and the potential to be hired by you when they graduate if they do a good job.

DEALING WITH YOUR BANKER

It would be ideal to get a banker that is familiar with your industry. Most are not. And bankers don't really care about your business except the extents that you can repay any loans and you can give them deposit business from which they generate fee income. Banks are also a business, and they are in business to generate income off of business accounts and loans. But some small local banks might actually care.

Most banks, especially local ones, are more apt to consider lending to someone with a longstanding personal banking relationship with them prior to the advent of the new business. So, you should put money from personal savings into the bank you will borrow from, so they can get to know you before you borrow from them for your business. For businesses, it is always wise to have a line of credit to draw against even if you don't yet need the money. And small local banks tend to have more interest in small business success; try them before the big banks.

During the economic meltdown of 2008-2009 General Motors and Chrysler both needed federal government bailouts. Their stockholders were wiped out and the government effectively took over both companies. This was the only way the more than 200,000 jobs they combined to provide would still be around once the economy settled down and righted itself. Ford did not take a bailout. Why? Because the leaders of Ford were insightful and at the very beginning of the crisis had already had in place nearly $20 billion (with a "B") dollar worth of available but unused credit lines with numerous banks and brokerages. This available cash lifeline, even though little of it was ever used, saved Ford's stockholders. And Ford stock's still Ford stock, dividend and all.

It is wise to always have a ready line of credit for your company even if you don't need the money right away. It is also prudent to borrow something against it; a small amount if you don't need funds, the least amount necessary if you do, and then pay it back promptly each month on an accelerated schedule. This proves to the bank that you can manage your credit and pay back your loans. This will lead to more trust, and higher credit limits on your credit line. That way, if someday you need a massive amount of funds relative to your business size, you might just have the line of credit to borrow it because you planned for it in the beginning when you didn't need it.

Getting to know your local bank manager, tellers, and loan officers, helps to create maintain bank confidence in you and your business. Trust is built up over time and people prefer to do business with those they know rather than those they don't know. Staying in touch with your banker. Remember, too, that there are different banks for different people, and for different businesses. They should be shopped like a suit of clothing or a hat; make sure they fit properly.

There are three important credit questions bankers are trained to look for. They involve Safety, Liquidity, and Income. First, is there sufficient collateral like receivables ("A/R" for accounts receivable), inventory, equipment, and real estate or leaseholds? Second, is there adequate liquidity? Does the business generate enough cash-flow that there is cash to pay bills? This is especially important in times of tight money or in an economic downturn. Third, is there sufficient Income? Income is the key metric to a banker to ascertain if you can pay back your loan. Lack one and you might get a loan, but lack all three and you never will. As long as you can prove or reasonably assure the bank that you can pay back the loan and the interest on the loan, you can generally obtain a loan. How much and for how long at what interest rate is determined by the safety, liquidity, and income components.

Banks evaluate your background to get an overview picture of what you've done in the past, your experience in your business field, your overall business background, your education, and your resources to use as collateral. They will draw credit reports (typically from Dun and Bradstreet, Robert Morris Agency and other credit agencies) on you and on your business to see what trade credit has been extended to your business in the past and if you have ever been involved in any defaults personally or professionally. Have you had overdrafts or bounced checks? Did you pay (and are you now paying) your debts on time? They will do lien searches and personal background checks, too. Some even perform criminal background checks where allowed by law. All of this is to determine if you are a good risk: defined as meaning you will likely pay the bank what you owe, and on time.

Always be honest and forthright in your disclosures to banks, insurers, and professionals that you hire to assist you. Never lie. This doesn't mean you have to disclose everything, but never lie about what you do tell; invariably those lies come out and the truth will too. Sooner or later, it catches up with you; don't let it, by not lying in the first place. It is better to tell the bad news as well as the good. This will only strengthen your relationship with your banker and other professionals. Be friendly. Be prepared to give a personal assets statement on what you own. And be ready to fill out lots of forms with invasive questions.

To get a loan (certainly for your first loan) you will probably have to make a personal guarantee to the bank for it. Bankers like to hear about the "bottom line" and returns on investments. You can often renegotiate your loan by noting the size, term length, and type of money needed, and pay some fees and come out with a new loan. Banks will review the loan agreement and go over all of the constraints including what collateral is needed. The rate you will be charged is important, so be prepared ahead of time by finding out what the interest rate is and determining ahead of time if you can afford to carry the loan at the interest rate to be charged.

They will also want to see a dynamite business plan that is well thought-out, detailed, predictive, and shows experience that thought went into it.

It will show the reader how the business will succeed, how long it will take to become profitable, how to address and resolve any and all problems, and how the bank (your "investor") will be paid back.

One of my banker friends once said: "Find the right bank and find a path to the top. It's difficult to deal with lesser branch officers, so the best strategy is to meet with a senior Vice President." He said, "A number of finance majors' first jobs out of colleges are as bank loan officers. Many that do nothing else for the first few years end up making it a career." While harsh, his view was that lower level loan officers have a parochial outlook and go "by the book" on everything.

I responded by saying that I disagreed with his view. I told him that I'd found most loan officers to be helpful and polite. But exceptions to any rule do happen.

So, can you switch banks? It's not easy, and for businesses it's not common to need to do, but it happens. Businesses shop their banks all the time looking for better terms. But what if you bank shops you and decides you're too big a risk, or your business is worth enough to them, or their policies have changed and now your loan doesn't conform to their underwriting requirements and you will have the loan "called" and have to pay it back right away? What do you do?

When a bank tells you they will not carry your loan anymore you need to have an alternative or you must repay without new funds to replace the loan. There are many reasons you might need a new bank. You have a serious disagreement with bank personnel on how they are handling your account. You believe another bank will charge less interest, or lower fees, or provide better terms than the current one does. Maybe you need and larger loan, can qualify, but your bank won't loan more due to either loan diversification policies in the bank or because they don't think you're creditworthy for a larger loan, but you need it anyway and think they're wrong? Maybe another bank has a package and it costs less. Sometimes it is the fact that many bank loans contain a covenant that prohibits owners from withdrawing more than a certain percentage of profit from the business, sometimes referred to as a "leave-in" clause. If they make you keep 50% of the profits in the business but you're paying taxes on that money you are building up assets in the business but can't touch it. A new bank might let you take 75% out instead of 50%. That's a reason to leave. (Almost all owners must withdraw at least enough to pay taxes annually since less than 1% of companies are C-Corps and taxes are due annually whether the money to cover them is distributed to the owners, or not.)

If you can work out your disagreements with bank personnel before changing banks it's better, but otherwise, it could reflect unfairly about your account in a negative way and affect your relationship with your new bank as a money source for you. Still, if you gotta go, you gotta go.

You can also use one bank's terms and rates to bargain with another. If the new bank believes you are a good risk and a profitable account, they may offer you better terms of lower rates and still come out ahead because your account is business they didn't have and they are stealing it from a competitor. That's a win-win for you and your new bank.

Loans from banks are basically using other people's money to finance your business. Instead of having to wait until you come up with enough cash, you borrow it. The cost of this is the interest rate you pay for the privilege of borrowing other people's money.

Partners are another way to use OPM to fund your business. If it is money that is not yours, it is by definition someone else's money. OPM is how you get a mortgage. Depositors put money in banks for some paltry interest rate. Banks lend it out to borrowers for a substantially higher rate, making a profit on the "spread" between what they pay to depositors and what they charge borrowers. OPM is used most often to buy real estate, as it is usually the largest purchase a person makes on a personal basis, and few have the money to buy a house for cash.

Issuing stock is another way to use OPM. They buy your stock for cash and they own a piece of the business, and of the equity and the profits.

All uses of OPM cost you something; nothing is free. Even barter has a cost (forget the tax ramifications for a moment) even when goods or services traded, or bartered, without money changing hands. Still, each side surrenders something. Nothing is free except bad advice.

Here's an example of a common START-UP small business loan pitfall:

A deal was brought to a bank lender on an electronics resale business. It was estimated that sales could be between one million and $1.5 million dollars a year. The person said he needed $150,000 cash to start it up.

Later it became known that he really needed another $100,000 more at the end of the year and needed 14 to 16 months before breakeven, not the originally promised 6 months. He lied. (Or he embellished and exaggerated.)

What he should have done is acquire sufficient knowledge of the business and finances needed before he started. An entrepreneur's biggest advantage is maneuverability. In startup equity, you must be able to go 18 months before making a profit, and you must have sufficient capital from DAY ONE to make sure you have enough cash to make it to that profit point.

RATIOS USED IN BUSINESS, AND FOR DETERMINING LOANS (formulas in *Italics*)

Profit Ratio. This measures earnings in relation to sales and investment.

Gross Margin Ratio. This is *"Sales - Cost of Goods Sold, then / (divided by) Sales."*

Net Profit Ratio. This is *"Net Profit (before taxes) / (divided by) Net Sales."*

Liquidity Ratio. This is quite simply the ability to pay bills as they come due from cash.

Current Ratio. This is *"Current Assets / (divided by) Current Liabilities."*

Acid-Test Ratio. This is *"Current Assets – Inventory, then / (divided by) Current Liabilities."*

Turnover Ratio. This shows asset effectiveness in generating sales and profits, and measures how many times in a year the inventory sells. Example: 20 in sales of 4 in inventory = TR of 5.

Working Capital Turnover. This is *"Net Sales / (divided by) Current Assets - Current Liabilities."*

Inventory Turnover. This is *"Net Sales / (divided by) Average Inventory carried at Retail cost."*

Leverage Ratio. This measures the amount of leverage, or multiple, creditor capital Investment as against capital contributed by owners.

Debt to Equity Ratio. This is "*fixed liabilities / (divided by) Tangible Net Worth.*"

You have to pay off fixed costs, including your loans. In order to determine the margin of monthly sales as it compares to paying off your expenses, follow these steps after you total all your fixed expenses for the month times 12 months: divide the total by the "unit margin" or profit per unit sold. "*Fixed Expenses per Period / (divided by) Profit Margin per Unit.*" Example: if you need $1000 per month toward fixed expenses, and you make $20 profit per unit, divide $1000/$20 and you get 50 units per month. This breakdown method works for all retail, wholesale and manufacturing businesses. You must know how much in gross sales you need to breakeven, **before** making a profit each month.

SAMPLE BREAKDOWN CHART ON OVERHEAD MONTHLY SALES

You can insert your own costs and expense numbers below; this is just a sample for instruction.

Profit Margin: $15 Per Unit. (Unit Cost: $25. Materials/Labor: $8. Other: $2. Net Margin: $15.)

Fixed Expenses Per Month: $18,000. (Rent: $5000. Utilities: $1500. Salaries: $6000. Overhead: $5500. Total Fixed Expenses Per Month: $18,000.)

Monthly Breakeven: 1200 Units. ($18,000 Fixes Expenses / $15 Margin Per Unit = 1200.)

In Chapter 9, we'll cover basics of income, asset, and balance sheets, and how you record and analyze all of the things you need to know to make sure your business will stay in business.

CHAPTER NINE
Finances, Balance Sheets, and Income Statements

How will you fund your start-up, and how will you make sure you survive financially long enough to become viable? While your Business Plan should identify your intended source(s) of funds, think about what other options you may have to finance your new endeavor.

First, let's talk about how you initially capitalize your venture. The so-called 'First Dollar' of funding. There are three primary ways. You can **front** the money, **borrow** the money, or **syndicate** the money; funding it yourself is the easiest and most common way to start a new business.

Fronting the money is the easiest to do (really?) because you don't have to prove to someone else that your idea is a winner, and you don't have to answer to anyone else with respect to how you spend it (no banks and no investors or partners). It is the hardest to do (really!) because most people starting a business don't have loads of extra cash just lying around to start a business unless they've been saving for it for years (or sell or cash out some major asset). It's always best if you can finance your business yourself, but most people cannot provide anywhere near all of the funds required out of their own money to start their business.

So, they **Borrow** the money. We discussed this before. Now this can be done in one of three ways. Owner loans, investor loans, and financed loans. Owner loans are monies borrowed by the owner of the business personally, not by the business from a bank or investor. The most typical two ways are with a personal credit card, and by using money from a HELOC (Home Equity Line of Credit) or a loan against some other major asset. As of 2018 HELOC interest cannot be deducted on individual tax returns unless the HELOC is used exclusively for repairs or upgrades to the home against which it is borrowed, so this has now become a method of last resort to fund a business. (Unless, of course, your HELOC loan is to modify your garage or home for a home-based business.) Most owners go the credit-card route since it's easy, they get points or cash back, and they are in control of the spending; until they max out the credit line and they're stuck with the bill, that (remember) goes against the owner's, not the business, credit record. (The owner is personally liable.) Remember, some personal credit cards ban use of personal cards for business purposes, which can result in cancellation of the card, if the issuer finds out you are using that arrangement.

Investor loans use other people's money, but this usually results in giving up anywhere from some, to a majority of operating and ownership control. Having outside investors means answering to them every time you make a major expenditure, which can be quite often. You have to justify everything you do, and if you deviate from your Business Plan in even the slightest way, you will encounter resistance from these investors. And they meddle constantly. It is rare for an outside investor to be silent and hands-off operations. Oftentimes, these investors are family members, friends, or the two or three people you left your job with to partner up and try to take your shot at the business world with. But when they are strangers, watch out, because they won't care whether you live or die, only whether they get repaid.

By the way, investors rarely invest unless the owner has also invested what is usually significant money into the business first. There is a saying "having skin in the game" that means that the owner has a lot to lose if the venture fails. Investors want the owner to lose a lot if they lose their investment, and so having skin in the game as the founder of the business is critical to getting outside investors to invest.

Financed loans usually mean bank loans, as in bank to business. In almost all cases with start-ups, a bank loan will not just involve the signature of the controlling officer of the company, but will also require the personal guarantee(s) of the owner(s)/borrower(s), who must pledge everything they own, including their house, car, savings, and personal belongings, as collateral for the loan. If the company fails, the guarantor is usually ruined. So, while the business is responsible for paying off the loan on time, any default by the business and the owner is usually on the hook, with no way to escape liability for paying off the loan. Banks are in the business of lending money they expect to get back, with interest, so unless you have lots of assets you can secure the loan against, it will be tough for a start-up that is not already well-financed to get bank loans unless they are cosigned by the owner and/or some other party who has the wherewithal to pay the bank back if the business does not, and pledges that collateral. There are of course other loans not provided by banks. These include Small Business Administration SBA Loans, Grants,

TIFF-financing (Tax Incremental Funds Financing), and private lenders who all can and do provide loans to start-ups based on their category of business, their ownership demographic, or some other measure. Add grants from local and state governments, and women and minority loans, and you get the idea.

Finally, there is **Syndicated** money. This takes two forms: stock offerings, and true syndication. The former involves having a business that is either big enough, profitable enough, or "it" enough to offer is stock to the public in. This is rare and practically unheard of for start-ups. Even companies like Facebook had to wait a few years before they could go public, and only after several rounds of investor funding.

True syndication, on the other hand, involves sourcing anywhere from a handful to dozens of early stage or "angel" investors who will take a risk with some small to medium valued investment for both a percentage of the new company, and a chance to be part of the "next big thing" to hit the market. Think of a start-up that makes high-end widgets that wants to finance itself by having, say, 100 pro-sports athletes invest $10,000 each and in exchange they not only get a fractional ownership share of say a quarter of a percent each but also get first right to buy one a new widget at a discount. Or maybe for their investment they instead get a $5,000 retail widget before the public plus their ownership share. That's a syndication. Or like Tesla's $1,000 Tesla-3 car reservation deposit; if you collect enough of these deposits you have your initial funding. Typically, these investors are sourced through a professional who finds investor groups and takes a fee or a percentage (like a broker) of the funds raised for successfully finding funding. (Note: this is usually a small investment advisory firm and not typically an investment bank like, say, Morgan Stanley, but it can be.)

Unless you have the kind of business idea that generally means investors flock to you first, which is rarer than a blue lobster, this is also a difficult way to raise initial capital for your start-up, and fraught with the problems of having not a few but a few hundred investors who all want answers yesterday and their share of the profits the day before.

These are all ways to raise funds. As to ongoing funding, such as Stage-2 (operations), and Stage-3 (marketing and expansion), and other level funding that occurs after your initial start-up in business, they will be discussed later.

- - - -

Socrates said "Know Thyself." This is as useful in small business as it is in our personal lives. A lot of changes are subtly taking place in the economy. We often fail to notice the signs that point to these changes in time, to affect their outcomes. But a careful look at where your specific trade is, and where it may be going, can highlight for you some of the changes you may want to speed up, slow down, or even deter, for your new small business

We have all heard companies that stand still inevitably fall behind. In the rapidly shifting patterns of modern business finance, this has never been more-true than today, when complex and often little-known methods of financing are available to you. The Small Business community as a whole is seeking not only financing options, but more specialized methods available to them.

Some of these methods include remortgaging, refinancing, interim financing, term loans, factoring and perhaps the most challenging special forms of equipment and service leasing.

For the market(s) you want to merchandise your products or services to will need a good financial forecast to estimate your cash needs for an initial twelve-month period when starting up a Small Business. That means fairly accurate, estimated figures for your cash needs, especially for your first year of operations. You can get a lot of trade information from public and private sources, trade associations and the state or federal government administrations. You can contact additional information from future potential customers in the field, as well from interviews with people or competitors in the trade. But do not make the mistake of thinking that this replaces a good, accurate forecast. And a willingness to forgo salary early on to conserve start-up cash.

Small Businesses, because of the nature of each different operation, have special economic requirements. They must, at times, make buys where and when they are available, and then beat the bushes for customers who can use their products. Enormous outlays can be tied up in inventories and slow paying or bad-debt accounts.

To do business nowadays you must have the money, (at least that's what your creditors say.) In fact, in banking circles the joke seems to be the only time you can easily borrow is when you have enough money in the first place. And who has that?

Everything revolves around money. Your spouses need their "weekly allowance" and your teenage kids need spending money for lunches and dates. Employees need their wages. Your creditors want their bills paid. Even your customers need money to pay you or you won't be able to sell to them because they won't be able to pay you.

Money is required to buy new (not to mention used) equipment, to expand, to acquire inventory, and to pay expenses. Everybody has money problems at one time or another. Let's look at the intriguing business of money. To establish a proper frame of reference to finance and money, some definitions which are generally acceptable in the practice of sophisticated finance should be briefly discussed.

Just what is finance? It could be defined as the act of providing the means of payment. But quite simply, finance is money and the handling of it. Businessmen and women have made fortunes on very little capital by knowing how to properly exploit it.

Many times, what we need isn't more money but more financial planning coordination with the other facets of business management.

LET'S EXPLORE FINANCIAL PLANNING

The following will explain to you about (1) Pro-Forma Statements, (2) Cash Budgets, and (3) Ratio Analysis (Percentages)

Pro-forma's are future estimates of how your small business will fare at some specific future time during the forthcoming fiscal year. They are part of your Business Plan but also are stand-alone projections, too.

A pro-forma small business income statement contains the following: an estimated gross sales level, less cost of sales, to equal gross profits. (Sales-Sales Costs = Gross Profit.) You then deduct operating expenses to get net income. (Gross Profit – Expenses = Net Profit.)

A pro-forma balance sheet gives you an estimate of how your small business will look like 6 months or a year from now. What do these figures mean on a Balance Sheet? It's very simple. Our accountant friends have set up a specialized vocabulary which in essence is a "picture of a company on one particular day," nothing more or less. It is not a reward of a year's operation. The assets are owned, the liabilities are owed, plus surplus and owner's equity. And they must add up to 0. Assets must equal liabilities in the accounting world.

A pro-forma cash budget gives you a picture as to estimate cash receipts and cash disbursements each month for a year. This gives you an idea of your cash-flow in and out of your business. It gives you a good idea of the liquidity of your business.

You can budget your cash-flows "in and out" of your business by correlating cash receipts and cash disbursements to sales. You are then in a position to determine loan and repayment schedules such as short-term funds for seasonal needs. In turn, this will give you a sales forecast showing normal seasonal patterns and peak sales months. For example, high sales with sluggish cash receipts, coupled with heavy customer buying would necessitate bank financing during that period. Cash-flows are important to the small business owner, just ask any credit lender.

Let me tell you about Bob. Bob went into business a little over a year ago. He was recently thinking of closing his small business. Why? He was running out of gas, so to speak. That "gas" - a shortage of cash - is referred to as the "cash-flow" of the business.

Bob had roughly $10,000 a month in sales in his first year in business. It cost him $5000 to make his products, so his gross profit per month averaged $5000. But, that profit had to cover his rent, and other operating costs, which were above that $5000 and cost him $7000 a month. His accounts receivables were past 45 days, meaning his customers weren't paying him on time, or at all. Bob was running out of cash despite making a lot of profit. What he needed was either more sales, or more cash to pay suppliers and employees. What could he do?

When people first go into business, it often takes a while to cover their costs. When people open a business, they should have enough cash to support losses until the business makes a profit. It generally takes between 12 to 18 months before this happens. This allows for the contingency that a customer or 50 might not pay on time, or that some won't pay at all.

Even experienced business people overlook cash-flow. Bob did. And without adequate cash-flow, he couldn't pay his bills. As a result, Bob faced bankruptcy even though he made a profit.

What is cash-flow? Simply stated, cash-flow is the amount of cash generated and spent in the business. It's Cash-In, Cash-Out, during a given period of time. If you don't get paid on time, whether monthly or yearly. A business has to have ample cash to pay creditors and employees on time. If you don't get paid on time, you begin to run out of money to operate your business.

Like a family budget, income has to exceed expenses. You must have enough cash to pay the bills when they are due. The alternative is that over time you will lose your house, your car, and everything else. In business, you could lose it all too, just like Bob was doing.

Bob couldn't pay his invoices on time. Half his money went into inventory, and more than half went to operations. It left him with a loss of $2,000 in cash per month, and he didn't have it. The amazing thing was he made great profits but couldn't pay his bills because of the cash-flow shortage from his accounts. When his suppliers weren't paid, they stopped delivering to Bob. So Bob was going bankrupt. With a great idea and a successful business. All because he couldn't manage his cash-flow. (Better cost control would have been nice, too.)

What solutions are there to manage cash-flow problems? I offer these six pieces of advice. 1) Manage cash-flow problems by setting up a pro-forma business plan that shows when you will need cash to pay your bills. 2) estimate when cash is needed due to seasonal, holiday and summer sales to determine cash-flow needed. 3) check your invoiced accounts receivables for prompt payments, by offering discounts for early payments, or get pre-payments with orders. 4) establish a bank line of credit before money is needed to cover cash shortfalls. 5) sell your accounts receivable to a financing company, called factoring. 6) offer discount incentives for early pay. Drop slow paying accounts.

So now, you know a little more about cash-flow. Bob did, and it ultimately saved his small business.

Everybody likes numbers, so let's talk numbers. Actually, percentages. Ratio percentages, that is. Ratio Analysis shows how you are heading financially by percentage comparisons - comparisons that is, to your fellow competitors. Various trade and business organizations have issued balance sheet ratio percentages on certain industries that could help you to see how you compare against your peers. If you are out of line on certain ratios it may pay you to revise your overall business operation to bring it more in line with the industry ratios. Such as if your inventory percentages are too high, it might mean an immediate reduction of inventory should take place. On the other hand, if your percentages are too low, perhaps your small business isn't utilizing proper business management in certain phases of your business.

Let's explore the Time Value of Money. A dollar a year from now is less valuable than a dollar today. Money depreciates, even just from inflation. The small business owner should put that dollar to work within their company now, so they can earn a current return on it.

What sources can a small business seek for financial assistance? There are many. Commercial banks, private bankers, equity (stock), sales partners, factors, insurance companies, SBA, Industrial Development Corporations, various City or State authorized loan services, friends, relatives, and even customers are all sources for financial help.

HOW IS YOUR MONEY SPENT ON STARING UP A SMALL BUSINESS OPERATION

You can fill in any items not listed, but it gives you a good start on your costs and expenses. This list is not complete or in any special order but indicative of the requirements for Projected Start-Up Costs & Ongoing Operating Expenses)

START-UP COSTS	OPERATING EXPENSES
Down Payments & Deposits	Rent & Utilities
Decorating & Renovations	Monthly Telephone & Utilities
Furniture & Fixtures	Salaries, Payroll Taxes, Benefits
Equipment & Machinery	Professional Fees (CPA, Lawyer)
Telephone & Internet	Advertising & Publicity
Printing & Copying	Material & Services
Office Supplies	Sales Commissions
Licenses & Permits	Maintenance & Repairs
Starting Inventory	Janitorial & Trash
Working Capital (6 Months Min.)	Inventory Production Costs
Contingency Funds	Dues & Subscriptions
Rent	Owner's Draw/Salary

YOU CAN GET PLANNING, MARKETING, MENTORING, AND NETWORKING INFORMATION FROM THESE SMALL BUSINESS ORGANIZATIONS AND WEBSITES:

Contact or visit these organizations for more information:

SBA -SMALL BUSINESS ADMINISTRATION (http://sba.gov)

SCORE (https:/www.score.org/)

BNI (http://www.bni.com)

Entrepreneurs' Organization (https://eonetwork.org/)

StartUp Nation (https://startupnation.com)

NFIB National Federation of Independent Business (http://www.nfib.com)

Industry & Trade Associations (http://www.marketing-mentor.com/pages/trade-list)

SMALL BUSINESS ASSOCIATIONS

Women's Business Development Center (https://www.wbdc.org/)

Minority Chamber of Commerce (http://minoritychamber.net/)

Visit or Join your Local Chamber of Commerce (https://www.chamberof commerce.com)

Minority Business Development Agency (http://www.mbda.gov/)

SBA office of Veterans Business Development (https://www.sba.gov/offices/headquarters)

Ashoka Social Entrepreneur Organization (https://www.ashoka.org/)

National Restaurant Association (http://www.restaurant.org/Home)

(all these web addresses were operational when this book was printed)

(Please note: The following charts are provided for informational purposes only. The Authors do not endorse one chart over another nor vouch for the completeness of the below charts.)

BALANCE SHEET & INCOME STATEMENT

BALANCE SHEETS show lenders, bankers and suppliers your Small Business's borrowing capacity. One side ASSETS, the other side is LIABILITIES. Your Business's NET WORTH is the final result; reflecting profit or loss.

INCOME STATEMENTS give you snapshot of your performance. They provide a method to estimate profit or loss for a chosen period. (Month, Quarter, or Year.) Income Statements show sales, expenses, operating profit (or loss), and net income (or loss).

CASH FLOW and **COST ANALYSIS** charts are also provided for your use. Feel free to use the sample forms below to estimate your assets, income, cash flow, and costs. (Note: These are only demonstration samples. Assets and Liabilities should be equal. Not all options appear below. Not all categories apply to all businesses.)

Trial Balance Sheet for the year ending (Month, Day, Year)

ASSETS		LIABILITIES	
Current Assets		**Current Liabilities**	
Cash	$_____	Accounts Payable	$_____
Accounts Receivable	$_____	Current Debt	$_____
Inventory	$_____	Taxes Payable	$_____
TOTAL CURRENT ASSETS	$_____	**CURRENT LIABILITIES**	$_____
Fixed Assets		**Long Term ("L-T") Liabilities**	
Equipment	$_____	Notes Payable	$_____
Furniture	$_____	Capital Stock (Equity)	$_____
Fixtures	$_____	Retained Earnings	$_____
Other	$_____	axes Payable	$_____
TOTAL FIXED ASSETS	$_____	**TOTAL L-T LIABILITIES**	$_____
TOTAL ASSETS	$_____	**TOTAL LIABILITIES**	$_____

(TOTAL ASSETS SHOULD EQUAL TOTAL LIABILITIES)

INCOME STATEMENT

For the year ending (Month, Day, Year).

REVENUE

Gross Sales	$_____	
Less: Returns & Allowances	$_____	
NET SALES		$_____

COST OF GOODS SOLD

Beginning Inventory	$_____	
add: Purchases	$_____	
Freight – In	$_____	
Direct Labor	$_____	
Indirect Expenses	$_____	
Inventory Available	$_____	
Less: Ending Inventory	$_____	
COST OF GOODS SOLD		$_____
GROSS PROFIT (LOSS)		$_____

EXPENSES

Administrative Expenses	$_____
Advertising	$_____
Amortization and Depreciation	$_____
Bad Debt	$_____
Bank Charges	$_____
Charitable Expenses	$_____
Commissions and Contract Labor	$_____
Dues, Subscriptions, Memberships	$_____
Employee Benefits & Medical	$_____
Insurance	$_____
Interest (Bank Loans)	$_____
Legal & Accounting Fees	$_____
Licenses and Permits	$_____
Miscellaneous (Uncategorized)	$_____
Office Expenses & Supplies	$_____
Payroll Taxes	$_____
Postage & Mailing	$_____
Rent & Property Maintenance	$_____
General Repairs and Maintenance	$_____
Telephone & Internet	$_____
Travel	$_____
Utilities	$_____
Vehicle Expenses	$_____
Wages	$_____

TOTAL EXPENSES	$_____
NET OPERATING INCOME	$_____

OTHER INCOME (LOSS)

Gain (Loss) on Sales of Assets	$_____
Interest Income	$_____
Investment Income	$_____
TOTAL OTHER INCOME	$_____

GRAND TOTAL NET INCOME (LOSS)	$_____

CASH FLOW STATEMENT

FILL IN THE BLANKS WITH YOUR OWN CASH FLOW FIGURES SO YOU CAN SEE HOW YOU ARE DOING

CASH FLOW

Net Income	$_____
Depreciation	_____
(increase) decrease in current Assets	
Accounts Receivable	_____
Inventory	_____
Income Tax refundable	_____
	$_____
Increase (decrease) in current liabilities	
Accounts Payable	_____
Accrued payroll and payroll taxes	_____
Corporate taxes payable	_____
Net cash provided (used) by operating activities	$____ _____

Continued on next page...

Cash Flows used in investment activities	
Purchase of equipment	$_____
Net book value of disposed equipment	_____
Net cash provided (used) by investment activities	$_____
Cash flows used by financing activities	
Proceeds from notes payable	_____
Payment of notes payable	_____
Reduction of additional paid-in capital	_____
Net cash provided (used) by financing activities	$_____
Net increase (decrease) in cash	_____
Cash beginning of year	_____
CASH at end of year	$_____

START-UP COST ANALYSIS

START UP YEAR FINANCIAL COSTS

Here are some item breakdowns you should consider in working up your costs for your Small Business operation.

Fill in the approximate costs and add in any items not listed, that you will need in your start-up costs.

EXPENSE	Year 1	Year 2	Year 3
Advertising	_____	_____	_____
- Postage	_____	_____	_____
- Production	_____	_____	_____
Bank Charges	_____	_____	_____
Insurance	_____	_____	_____
Office Supplies	_____	_____	_____
Accounting	_____	_____	_____
Legal	_____	_____	_____
Computer/Phone	_____	_____	_____
Copy & Print	_____	_____	_____
Answering Service	_____	_____	_____
Rent & Utilities	_____	_____	_____
Salaries, Payroll Taxes	_____	_____	_____
Licenses & Permits	_____	_____	_____
Maintenance	_____	_____	_____
Sales Commissions	_____	_____	_____
Janitorial & Trash	_____	_____	_____
Dues & Subscriptions	_____	_____	_____
Transportation	_____	_____	_____
Miscellaneous	_____	_____	_____
GRAND TOTAL $$$	_____	_____	_____

CHAPTER TEN
The Next Step — Where Do You Go From Here?

You planned for a new business, went through the steps to set it up, got funding, made a go of it, and now you are in business. You overcame your biggest challenges with hard work and a good business plan, and now are making sales, **and money**. We discussed all this earlier, and now, perhaps, these few stories will give you some ideas in starting a business, merchandising a product or service, finding economical locations, and other tricks and advice from other businesses that have successfully used these methods and been profitable.

These real-life stories talk about compliances needed for your small business startup, by who to contact, when to do it and what to do to be an outstanding business owner.

IT TAKES PLANNING TO OPEN A SMALL BUSINESS

This is a perfect time to remind the "business wannabe" what they need to do to establish a small business and the types of things they should do to prepare prior to the opening day. Andrew owned a small business in Maine, a retail copy center. Like many New Englanders, he set up shop in his garage. A large number of Maine and other New England small businesses are home or garage based, which doesn't mean occasional sales on the Internet. Nope, there was a separate phone line, separate electric meter, and for one part, separate heat. There was a separate dedicated air conditioner to cool the machines. And there were a quarter of a million dollars' worth of copy machines (Andrew bought them at auction for pennies on the dollar; you can save like this too). The garage was separated from the house and run and set up entirely for the business. Expenses were made to refurbish it, build platforms and shelving and a cashiers' counter, and all of the other things needed to make it a thriving business. The office area was dedicated to just that business. [*Hint: I worked hard enough and did well enough that when I sold the business because I'd decided to attend law school, I sold the business and the property, in separate transactions, and made enough just in profit to pay for three years of law school. Hard work really works!*]

183

With this in mind, let's start at the beginning.

First, you'll need a business plan. A detailed, comprehensive, well-defined Plan. This expanded outline of the nature of your proposed business describes the types of customers and products to be sold, and the way you intend to do business. Marketing, sales, equipment acquisition and where to get the money are also described in the Plan. Of course, no Plan tells you everything, but it is a necessary roadmap to how you intend to be successful. Without a Plan, most businesses fail almost instantly. Of course, a good Plan won't save a bad idea, or make you rich by itself, but it is a guideline without which you cannot be reasonably assured to succeed.

Most people can make up their own Plans, but professionals will design one for a fee. [*Andrew has done that for clients. But they ain't cheap, so try to do it yourself, first. Otherwise, call me, we'll talk......*]

Second, you need a "concept" as well as a product. What will you sell? Do you have a unique product? Is it something people want or need? How will you acquire or make your product in short supply? It is readily available elsewhere in your market i.e. is it a commodity or if you are selling a product, you need to know that the market will support the product? If manufacturing a product, be sure you can make enough to reach economies of scale, and of course, be sure there are enough potential customers. Make sure you can buy or make your product at a cost low enough that when you sell (or resell) it that you can make a profit and pay all your bills.

Probably the most common reason new small businesses fail is money: more specifically, the lack of it. Some small business owners don't have enough in the beginning or they don't make enough money to cover expenses and pay salaries. Or they draw out too much salary and bleed the business of cash. Whatever the case is, the general rule of thumb is that new businesses invariably lose money for the first 18 months of operation. In other words, sales won't be high enough to cover costs for the first year and a half. Most businesses seriously underestimate the amount of money they will need during this time.

Assume that the owner — you — will not draw a salary for the first 6 months, and then decide if it is worth it to continue. (You must have a reserve of personal cash; it must be able to support you without a salary draw for up to 18 months.) If you have a good concept or great product, it usually is worth continuing. And if no one else in the area provides it, great!

So back to the garage. Most businesses have a storefront: a physical office location they own or rent, from where they conduct their business. It is relatively easy (but not necessarily cheap) to set up shop in your garage. This is common in Maine. (We use Maine because both Bernard and Andrew set up businesses there, and know the business climate.) Just look at the signs on the roads that point to a business: "Bill's Buds 1-1/2 miles" down the road. Bill's flower shop may have two coolers and a cash register in his garage, which was converted to a business, but it has a separate phone, power and Internet lines, as well as separate heat and A/C. And, it has been inspected by the town and has business licenses, permits, and a sales tax collection number with the State. In short, it's no different than if you rented a storefront.

Never forget that to run a business you will need those governmental approvals and licenses. You will need to register your business with your own State (or any state you intend to do business in). In Maine, http:www.maine.gov.portal/business/starting.html provided good links and information on how to incorporate your business, get revenue and tax licenses and where and how you can information on drafting your own business plan.

You will need a Tax Identification Number ("EIN Number", for Employer Identification Number: a social security number for your business, if you will) from the IRS; the irs.gov website has lots of forms and information but you will need to call in on the phone to get your EIN #, since it is not available online. Also, you will need state and local government registrations, licenses, and permits. If your state or city has sales taxes, you will need a sales tax collection number and a sales tax permit to collect these taxes for forwarding to the state or city. Building and Occupancy Permits are always local or county issued. Corporate names and registrations are always at the state level. And you cannot get an EIN number without a state corporate registration number and the date your business started; which is not when you opened your doors but the date on which the state recognized and approved your corporate form. Finally, you will need utilities and the like, and this requires having a bank account or other means to pay, so open that small business bank account once you get your EIN#.

Remember that except in rare instances, you will do all of this months before you actually make or sell anything. On average, a new business takes 60-90 days before they can open their doors from formation (state registration of your company name and form) until they begin manufacturing or selling anything. Incorporate this fact into your plan and be prepared that for the first 3-4 months, there will be NO revenue and only expenses.

SMALL BUSINESS OWNERS MUST LEARN MARKETING, PRICING AND ADMINISTRATION

Surely, many of you have been to a "grand opening" of a new business. They have balloons, prizes, a few freebies, entertainment, and great sales. You may have gotten some of these goodies yourself. But who paid for them? The new business, that's who; it's a marketing cost. How you get customers is one of the most important things you need to know, other than how to manage revenues and expenses so you don't go bankrupt. Most small businesses are retail, selling services or products to a final buyer, not like a manufacturer sells to a store. You might sell to stores too, but most retailers don't. So how many customers you get through your door every day to come in and buy from you is critical. How you get them is through Marketing.

Marketing is the process by which businesses promote themselves to potential customers. Sometimes, an ad in a newspaper, sometimes direct mail, sometimes via TV or radio ads, or sometimes through a Google search ad. It depends who your target market is. If you market to businesses, then direct mail, phone calls, physical cold calling and what I call "relay" marketing may work best. Relay marketing is where you "piggyback" on someone else to relay your ad message for you. Perfect examples are mail or newspaper inserts. Newspapers, Chambers of Commerce, and other organization newsletters and bulletins "marry" together with other similar mail to provide good distribution at reasonable "per-viewer" rates. Broadcast TV and radio provide wider distribution but at a higher cost per viewer. Direct mail is more personal, although it has a higher per-viewer cost and can be cumbersome to produce, and is often discarded as "junk mail." Response rates vary, from fractions of a percent on radio and TV to about 1%-2% on direct mail. 1.5% is considered great, 5% unheard-of.

And remember this sobering statistic: historically, 96% of the people who leave your establishment without buying, even if they say they'll be back, never return or buy anything. That's 24 of 25! Only some 4% come back. This means that "foot" traffic - customers coming to you and how you get them to do so - is critical to your business's survival.

Some good ways to get new business are sales, promotions, and events. Sales are a lowering of prices of some or all goods, for a limited time, to entice people to buy. Remember that if you advertise a sale, you must follow through with sufficient stock on hand at that price. Governments look closely and angrily at businesses that do not honor sale prices. Promotions are price-lowering tricks that get people to buy without a "sale." Perfect examples of promotions are coupons, BOGO's (buy-one-get-one free or at a discount), percent-off deals, and "tie-ins" (where you buy "A" and get "B" free or at a discount). An example of an Event is a "tent sale" where the store brings in extra or special products not regularly available or displays products onsite or outside the front door so buyers can sample or test them. Events are intended to be visible so they create desire among passersby to want to view the goods for sale. Sales work best with products that rarely discounted, but have high profit margins. Promotions work because they get people to choose a coupon deal over a sale for the same discount (department stores are the classic example) because of the perception that it is a better deal. Events work best with unique, large scale, or difficult to handle products like appliances or technology items, or when you hold a "once-a-year" sale for a week as a regular annual event to be known for promoting in that week; this drives customers to wait and come to the event, which is also a deficit in that it can postpone sales until the event takes place.

Some customers are attuned to discounting and will only buy with one. They wait for the sale. The best example of this is the supermarket weekly flyer. Shoppers will want until the food they want is put on sale, and they know certain categories like bread, soda, and meats go on rotational sales every few weeks. Each week something different is on sale, and they wait for what they want. This postpones some purchases until they are discounted, which isn't always good for the business. But it drives unit sales more than dollar sales, and sometimes generates enough volume to overcome the sale discounts.

This leads us to Pricing. Most products sold today are marked up from wholesale (the price the store pays) to retail (the price the consumer pays). Markups range from 3 percent (most new autos) to double or more (many consumer goods). The actual markup depends on the industry, the product, the seller, how they are sold, and how much profit a store wants to make per item. The key is to make sure you price your products or services such that you make a sufficient profit. Not so high that you can't compete, but high enough to cover your costs and make some extra. Always remember: you are in business to make a profit, so never price to make a loss!

And never compete against yourself. That means never discount if you don't have to.

Finally, there is Administration, or the "back-office" of your business. Here are seven recommended precepts: One, have "at the ready" good accountants and lawyers. Use accountants to prepare your statements and taxes even if you have a bookkeeper and a financial controller. Do as much prep work yourself as possible to lower professional costs. An Attorney is useful for contracts and complex documents and to review leases (if you have one), initial permitting, variances, licenses and when problems occur, which they invariably will. Two, keep good clean "books" – ledgers of revenues and costs. And keep all records for at least 7 years to comply with most laws. And you can have more than one set of books and still not be a cheat. In fact, most businesses have two sets: a tax (payables/receivables/accruals) set and a cash (flow) set.

Each set records things differently for different reasons, but both are legal. And, in the end, the bottom line is the end-of-day numbers in both will always match.

Three, deal with vendors/suppliers yourself, don't delegate unless you've hired a purchasing agent employee to do the job. Four, hire trustworthy workers who show up on time and do a days' work for a days' pay. Pay Them Fairly. Pay them enough that they want to work for you, and will want to be loyal to you. Five, do not overbuy on your office supplies or sales inventory. Six, banks can be a great help, not just for funds, but for merchant services (credit card processing, for example) and for business networking. And, Seventh and lastly, always join your Chamber of Commerce, if there is one. They provide opportunities for networking that lead to new business, from other businesses, that you never would have gotten otherwise.

SMALL BUSINESSES ARE NOT EVIL AND DESERVE TO MAKE A PROFIT

Most businesses in America are small businesses. There are approximately 28 million small businesses; 22 million of them are one-person businesses with no employees. (The Census Bureau reported that in 2010 there were 27.9 million small businesses - and 18,500 with more than 500 employees, which account for nearly every publicly traded company.) Small businesses are the backbone of our economy and responsible for the bulk of net new jobs, according to the Small Business Administration. In order to create those jobs, small businesses need profits to exist.

Many people think small business owners make lots of money and so they should share some of it with others. Some people even think small business owners get rich. Yes, there are the Gates and Buffets and Zuckerbergs who made fortunes seemingly overnight from one big idea and now are wealthier than most countries, but no one actually sees the hard work they put into their venture and the risks they took with everything they owned on the line before they "made it" big. Small business owners work hard and long hours to get the benefit of their labor. They really deserve their wealth should they be amongst the very few who actually get some.

When things get tough in difficult times, small business owner's profits go down, because they get fewer orders. When they cut or don't pay a salary, it is theirs that is the first to be put on hold. One reason for sales declines is that unemployed workers have less money to buy goods and services from small businesses. Sometimes it seems the first thing that government, both local and federal, wants to do is to clamp down and squeeze the profits from small businesses, by instituting excessive product and factory regulations, increasing business taxes, and placing unnecessary controls on operating small businesses.

Small businesses are a minority group in this country. Large in number, but small in individual power. Most can't afford to hire lobbyists to help them because they don't have deep pockets that big companies have. They also do not have the power of the unions.

Small business owners can be outvoted in the political arena on laws affecting their business, yet small business people continue positive results by working harder and being more convincing than other people. Most taxes or unnecessary regulations are easy to pass it on to small businesses. They are usually the safest small group of political voters to burden. Some voters want more governmental services, as long as someone else pays for them. And it usually falls to small and medium sized businesses to pay.

When small businesses and their workers are at odds, the political system is often slanted towards labor, not because labor is inherently more worthy, but because there are so many more workers than owners of small businesses. Politicians frequently capitulate to organized workers in government, because they need their support to get reelected. This is why public employees often are paid more than what private industry employees earn for the same work.

Government officials have suggested for years that making profits without sharing them is immoral. It is true that some business people are very wealthy, but that is not true of the average small business owner. Business people generally work long hours to earn a decent living. They don't get rich until or if they sell their business and retire, and even then, most never get rich. They do not control the costs of their supplies, and have to pay their employee's wages and salaries that are competitive to what those workers could earn elsewhere.

Even when their costs go up, small businesses may not always be able to raise their prices proportionally and still attract buyers. So why are wages thought to be subject to some cherished and immutable law that says they must always go up, in good or bad times?

Small businesses profit by outworking and out-planning people who don't make the same effort, or are afraid to take the risks of going into business. Without profits, no one would invest money or time in any business venture, ever. The question often asked by small business owners is why should people with less income share in their hard-earned profits, without taking the same kind of risks? A person in business must be given an incentive to invest, to innovate, to sell their products or services at a fair profit in order to survive. Profits are not a dirty word. The extent of much anti-business legislation being talked about today is in the direction of controlling not only prices, but profits as well. Taking this away, through estate or wealth taxes, or by regulation, just makes people say "why the hell should I break my back and neck to make it only to have the government take it away" and if this happens business will grind to a stop. Don't you agree that if you slave for 10 or 20 years to build a business that you deserve any wealth that you amass from it? Sure you do. That's why there are businesses in the first place: because there is a profit incentive to do so.

Small business owners must get out and do something about it. It is a no-brainer to agree that profit is necessary for businesses to exist.

WORKING WITH EXPERTS AND PROFESSIONALS

I know when it is necessary or prudent to hire a pro to do the job. Please note that if I mention specific brands or products it is not an endorsement, just an example.

All businesses, at some point, have to file tax returns, pay salaries, and deal with government regulations. They have to incorporate, interact with government agencies, get approval from authorities, and perhaps even defend against or institute a lawsuit: people may claim to slip, fall and injure themselves on business property. Each occasion requires some expertise that may be beyond that of the average business owner. So, when do you hire a professional to do something for you?

Deciding to hire a professional is a three-step process. First you need to determine if you lack the expertise; does the expert you are considering have substantially more than you? Second, you have to balance the cost of experts against the extra benefits they confer. Third, you have to find the right expert to do the job for you.

Accountants are almost a requirement in business, especially manufacturing and retail firms. Larger firms hire bookkeepers and controllers, who perform most of the accounting functions, including tax returns, payrolls, payables, receivables and financial "control" (the art of balancing all these financial interests while collecting monies due and paying bills at the last possible minute) to maximize cash-flow. Public companies must hire outside (non-employee) accountants to produce and "audit" financials to comply with reporting laws like Sarbanes-Oxley.

Private, small and sole-proprietorship businesses may be able to use programs like Quicken to do their taxes, payrolls, or other simple financial documents. But if you have dozens or hundreds of employees, you may want to hire an accountant for financials, and a payroll service for weekly payrolls. (Most states require wages must be paid to employees weekly, unless you fall under a special exemption like lawyers or educators who are sometimes permitted to be paid monthly or bi-weekly.) Most accountants, like attorneys and other professionals, charge by the hour. Some charge flat fees for certain services. Payroll services charge a combination fee based on the number of employees they make checks for plus a flat service charge per pay period. To minimize costs, do as much of the prep work yourself as you can, like keeping good "books" – ledgers of sales and expenses, payroll and employee wage and hours information, and other records and documents for your business.

Attorneys can help you write and review contracts, leases, and other documents. They can represent you in permitting, variance and license processes or hearings; they can even incorporate your business for you. But perhaps the best reason to have an ongoing relationship with a lawyer is so they can advise you how not to have problems, before they happen. As an attorney, the primary duties to the clients is to give them good advice; to advise them how to avoid the kinds of problems that would cause them to hire the attorney in the first place, as much as to "problem-solve" once such problems occur. Attorneys charge by the hour, although some cases may be accepted on contingency; this is where the attorney agrees to charge a percentage of the recovery or award only if they win the case and there is an award or recovery. Some attorneys charge flat fees for certain services. Be sure to ask. [*As an attorney, Andrew knows first-hand that the best lawyers don't resolve client problems, they provide the good advice and counsel to their clients to keep those clients from having any major problems in the first place.*]

Your Better Business Bureau or Chamber of Commerce can give you names of professionals who are members, and sources such as the Yellow Pages or the Internet can be useful to search for local experts. Word-of-mouth from friends and colleagues is also a good source. Remember to always get a clear explanation of, and negotiate all, fees and terms prior to hiring them. Make sure your contract with them states what they do, what they will not do, and covers all other important terms and conditions. And don't waste their time because they charge a lot - and usually in 6-minute increments.

"MUST" BUSINESS SERVICES

All businesses should have insurance covering them against theft, liability, business interruption losses, and damage. Any business that does not carry basic insurance is stupid (yes, stupid) and asking for trouble, as just one claim can seriously damage or even bankrupt the company. And it really happens; it's not just a scare story.

Whether you use an insurance broker or contract directly with the underwriter (the insurance company itself), you should have at least a basic policy that covers you for the following: property damage (as owner or renter), liability (to protect against slip-and-fall or other injuries), fire and casualty, theft, employee bonding (if they handle money or valuables), and business interruption (which replaces your regular revenues if the business stops operating because of some insured problem). Insurance brokers usually get a percentage of your premiums, which are set by the underwriters, not the brokers; so the premium you are quoted is generally what you pay. Premiums do vary by broker and underwriter, so shop around. Independent brokers who do not write policies for just one underwriter are best, but be careful because different underwriters may pay different percentages to the broker. If you find a good insurance broker you like, you usually can stick with them long term, and many businesses have the same accountants, lawyers, and insurance brokers or agents for decades (if they last that long).

Previously, I mentioned payroll services. ADP, Paychex and others provide payroll and other services, including printing checks, calculating payroll taxes, 401(k) plans, and calculating deductions and tax deposits, as well as other services. They are easier than printing in-house unless you are huge, and their fees usually cost you less than if you had to hire someone to do it as an employee. Certainly, cheaper than hiring a bookkeeper (or doing it yourself) for businesses from about 10 to 50 employees, give or take a few. Sole proprietors, small partnerships, and subchapter-S businesses with only one employee may be better off doing their payrolls themselves, although it is best to ask your accountants for their advice.

As simple as it seems, photocopies are a big issue for businesses. Most copiers leased, because high-volume machines are too expensive and lease costs can be expensed for tax purposes. You pay a monthly rental, which includes all toner, and service calls, and provides a certain number of "clicks" or copies per month. All you pay for is the paper. Unless you make fewer than 25 copies a day, lease, don't buy. You may think that laser printer is a great copier but is cannot handle 15,000 copies in a month. [*I know, Andrew owned a copy center, remember?*] The same goes for major equipment unless it is of a type that is generally owned. But coffee, water and food services cannot be expensed for tax purposes, so they should be hired for convenience of employees or per-use costs only. Office supplies – especially paper – should be delivered. Most office supply companies will still deliver free if the order is over a certain amount. And of course, remember not to overbuy office supplies!

Telephones should be multi-line with speakers and hold buttons. Get a calling package that closely matches your calling pattern. Most phone companies (there are more than one; cable now provides VOIP lines to businesses) will do a free analysis to help you pick the right plan. Computers should be purchased, not leased, and virus protected! At least one primary business operations computer should be separate from the rest and not on the internet to prevent infection. And follow this rule about your corporate computers without fail or exception: **NEVER LET OUTSIDERS USE THEM. EVER. NO EXCEPTIONS!!!** Internet plans should include sufficient bandwidth for your business needs. Desks and chairs should be comfortable and functional. Don't cheap out on these things. And back-up data daily.

Establish relationships with local banks. Banks provide both deposit and payroll accounts, as well as making loans so that you can fund or expand your business. Banks provide "merchant services" like credit and debit card processing. Some negotiate fees, and some have business accounts with flat (or no) fees that package service services together. Remember how I said banks can be evil and don't care about you? That's only partly true. Some bankers establish long and lasting good relationships with business clients. As long as both sides are fair and honest with each other, there's no reason not to work with, and not against, each other. Banks lend to business and business pays fees to banks. Where one causes the benefit of the other, both sides win.

If you send out 500 or more letters a month, you may want a Postal Machine, like a Pitney Bowes. It prints postage on envelopes (after you pre-deposit funds with the Post Office), saving you from lost stamps. It also saves time - instead of manually putting stamps on your 1,000-mailer promotion. It is also good policy to get a P.O. Box for customers to send payments to. That way, no mail gets lost, it's safe, access is restricted, and you always get it at the same time each day.

Many businesses hire janitorial services to clean weekly or on some other schedule. This is good where you have high traffic and lots of trash. Or, you can clean toilets yourself and save money. Ugh!

Finally, be aware that this is not an exhaustive list. The library or local bookstore has books on starting a business, and the Chamber of Commerce can give you help too. After all, their job is to help local member businesses do more business!

SMALL BUSINESS OWNERS SHOULD BE LEADERS IN THEIR COMMUNITIES

Leadership makes a difference, as any small business that has experienced near death and then been turned around, can attest to. Whether it is applied in a business or a non-profit setting, strong leadership produces results. In today's world, leaders need to articulate a mission and future vision for their organizations, ones that can produce positive results.

Ownership is not automatically leadership. Owning a company may give a person the ability to call some shots, but it certainly does not guarantee present or continued success.

Successful leaders have learned that there is nothing constant but change, especially in this present economic recession. A good leader needs to do several important things, to keep an organization stabilized in such an unstable environment as we face right now.

First, employees of an organization need to know what is happening in the marketplace. Employees read newspapers and listen to radio and television news reports. If the boss does not offer information about the company's status, employees will fear that the place is really in deep trouble. Secrecy about financial well-being, at a time like this, will not inspire confidence: it will breed fear.

Second, the people who work for a business need to believe that the senior managers are honest and fair. If they are perceived as honest, then when news is shared, it will be believed. If they are seen as fair, staff will be less afraid of abrupt layoffs, or favoritism taking place. People work harder for managers they trust.

Thirdly, good leaders have plans, and not just for the short term. The short term grows into the long term, and companies have to prepare for what they will be ready to do when the market improves. If you wait until the customers all have money to spend, before you have new products for them, when the economy starts to ride high again, the customers will head straight for someone else's brand-new items.

Fourth, to be a great leader, you must inspire people. You do that by setting an example by working hard, by demonstrating loyalty, by giving your customers or clients 110 percent effort, and by valuing the people you supervise.

Great leaders also take risks. They do not risk other people's money that has been entrusted to them, the way some recent Ponzi-scam artists have done. They risk their own time, talent and financial resources on ideas for building better products or developing better services for people. Great leaders dream big dreams, and act on them, instead of just thinking about them.

Many people think leaders are people who were lucky. They think leaders got where they are because they had money or lucky breaks. Some may have, but, in fact, most just got to the top with elbow grease. They earn their reputations by working hard and long hours, and pursuing ethical, high standards for their industry peers to follow. They built businesses through their dedication to their organization's survival and growth, and they did it mainly by deeds, rather than words alone.

Most of the successful leaders care about their communities, too, not just their jobs, products and services. They are motivated with a caring passion to do the right thing, at the right time for others. Smart leaders build networking bases, both internally for ideas and implementation, and externally to gain information, friendship and future business. And a great many successful leaders want to give back to their communities. These are the role models for leadership.

Leaders in small businesses and non-profit businesses are alike in many ways. They plan their goals for completion, one step at a time. If you are not yet a leader, but would like to eventually become one, you can learn how leadership works by volunteering at one of the many non-profit organizations in this area, and observing leaders in action.

You will find it is the first stepping-stone towards building new friendships and towards networking with community leaders that can help you become a future leader one day. It is worth the effort. Try it and see for yourself.

SMALL BUSINESSES SHOULD BAND TOGETHER TO SURVIVE

Sometimes small business owners have to solve complicated problems for survival, by thinking about the unthinkable. We need to face life or business changes that may permanently reorient the way we function or manage our lives. We need to think about what those changes might be and how we will deal with them. Knowledge about uncommon experiences and also the potential changes can help us to prepare for the future.

Years ago, my closet friend, a dedicated surgeon, told me about a four-day medical seminar he attended in Chicago. Surgeons went there to learn about rare surgical cases, not normally seen or properly diagnosed because of their rarities. One such case involved surgery on an abnormal complication of the hand needing a special surgical technique to prevent the loss of the hand.

As luck would have it, about a month following the Chicago seminar, a patient was referred to him on a similar case that he had reviewed. He made the right diagnosis on the patient's hand, utilizing the surgical technique he had learned. As a result, the patient's hand was saved. Knowing about the uncommon had proved its value.

Small business success is a product of a variety of past experiences, affecting the owner's everyday life and economic well-being. Rather than reinventing the wheel all over again, small business owners normally feel that if something worked in the past, people should stick to what they have done successfully and not change what they do.

But small business owners have to start thinking about uncommon opportunities that face them now, and the changes quickly heading their way. Business connections are now made through a world of computerization, smartphones, Internet communications and social networking. It is a world of sophisticated web specialization.

Robot automation in manufacturing has reduced human labor. This has increased productivity for manufacturers, but has cost jobs for workers. Internet retailing is rapidly increasing, as more and more people order supplies online. Online sales are only growing.

The next big marketing change will involve the public dealing directly with computers, instead of salespersons or clerks, in many stores and businesses. It's happening now every time you call customer service at you bank or cell phone company, among others. "Voice Recognition Systems" they are called. The future predictions are that you will buy groceries in a supermarket without a person at the register ("Amazon Go" Stores?) or do your banking without tellers to take deposits or cash checks (the ever-present ATM). It will be happening soon in many retail operations.

Future trends will push larger business operations, rather than small, individually owned businesses. It will be a world of "super order takers." There will be a decreasing number of local small businesses serving the end users. Big business brick and mortar retail stores will slowly disappear from shopping centers nationwide.

Big businesses will own their own domestic and foreign outlets for competitiveness and for volume sales. The large surviving independent retailers will establish local "mom and pop" small business outlets, to service the small end users that are not profitable for big businesses.

It will become an industry of giant retailers, since the largest, strongest businesses shall inherit each trade. It will be harder to be a small business in the future because of the tremendous buying power needed.

One solution is for small businesses to band together, in cooperatives for competitive buying and selling their goods. They need to pool their talents. Better buying and selling power leverage could give small businesses a cutting edge, by pooling financial and marketing knowledge, selling a wider range of products, at lower prices from volume buying.

First class education in management decision making, as well as online sales expertise, is needed in order to finance and control inventory. Consolidation can result in huge savings of paperless records, reduced office and warehouse employee staff, but encourage team loyalty that will build greater efficiencies and profit abilities for survival.

A lot of small businesses won't merge, but those that don't will eventually fold up and slowly disappear. A limited amount of "mom and pop" businesses could survive as pickup and exchange franchise stores for local Internet customers buying from big businesses. Other small businesses could grow to be super big businesses, too, by joint ventures, acquisitions or internally generated growth.

We need to read the signs of change to make it work for us. It is coming on fast. The future we face is one we will help to make ourselves.

SMALL BUSINESS OWNERS SHOULD NEVER GIVE UP

Courage and fortitude in small business takes many forms, just like in our private lives. Let me tell you a story about Johnny, who grew up with that kind of courage.

Johnny was handicapped. But you would never know it. He learned that to be a friend, you had to treat others with mutual respect. You had to care about each other. You had to do to others, as you would want them to do to you.

People used to stare at Johnny wherever he went: in school, at social events or just traveling to places. His handicap was a metal breathing tube in his throat, caused by a horse accident, which resulted in Johnny, at age seven, being unable to breathe through his nose or mouth. A few parents at his public elementary school even refused to have their children in the same class as Johnny because of his metal breathing tube. They were prejudiced against someone looking so different being around their child. How sad for all concerned.

People can be cruel and mean-spirited, not only as adults, but to children, too, without even realizing what they say or do can affect someone else's feelings in a hurtful way. Sometimes all of us do things without thinking about the other people's feelings. In a way we are all handicapped by doing that to others.

Johnny knew why people looked at him so strangely. He was different with the metal tube in his throat. But he was determined to overcome his handicap. He set a goal to be the very best person he could be, to excel at whatever he did. To succeed to life by leading a normal life in the future. And he did.

He learned to talk and sing songs by holding his finger over the breathing hole in the tube. He acted in school plays, even though he could only talk when he blocked off air coming out of his tube. He studied diligently in school. He learned because he was self-driven to do so. Education and friends were important to him. Johnny took over chores with a strong sense of responsibility, just as each of your children should do.

Then, 13 years later, Johnny's (and his parents') dream came true. He was cured by a surgeon using a new type of laser medical operation on his throat. Today, Johnny is normal. He speaks normally like you and me. He breathes normally through his nose and mouth. The tube was gone. (He still doesn't swim, though.)

After college, Johnny went on to be a television commentator on a local TV station and became a leading expert in the field of privacy. He worked for a Fortune-500 company. He ran for public office. Presently, Johnny lectures at a university and teaches others about real estate and privacy. And he is a real estate broker. All in all, a great success story.

As a small business owner, Johnny taught me that the world was an exciting place in which to live, even when you are handicapped. He taught me, as a businessperson, it is always too early to quit. He taught me to never, ever give up and that you can accomplish anything if you make your mind up to do it. That changed my outlook on life and it can change yours. In my mind, Johnny typifies what courage and fortitude truly represent.

Johnny's story should motivate you as a small business owner to do the very best you can in whatever you want to do. You can, like he did, get great satisfaction in doing what people say you cannot do, to be successful in business and in life.

Never, ever give up. Just ask my son Johnny.

CHAPTER ELEVEN
Jack's Axioms – 32 Rules For Getting Business

Jack Finley, a veteran, businessman, and former chair of the board of Westbrook College, and I became friendly in the late 1990's. At the time, I mentioned that I wanted to write a book on business, and he gave me his "Jack's Axioms" rules and said that if I wanted, I could feel free to include them in my book. I was so busy with other things I didn't get around to writing that book until much later, like now. Sadly, Jack died before he could see his words in print in my book. This is that book. So here are "Jack's Axioms- 32 Rules for Getting Business" that apply to both small and large businesses alike, verbatim.

Every one of the thirty-two rules given below was based on actual events which occurred in Jack Finley's professional life. Someday, he said, if he ever got the time and enthusiasm, he might have filled in the blanks. He'd love that I finally published them for him. And he lives on through his words of wisdom, which I hope will aid you in your quest to be successful in whatever future business you decide to start.

1. **Keep your ego out of the business.** There is a basic incompatibility between decisions made for the sake of personal gratification and those made for the sake of good business. Always keep someone around who isn't afraid to tell you that you are full of shit.

2. **There is no need to hurry.** If the Republican Congress had been willing to make a large victory out of a lot of small ones over time, they could have redefined government without anyone getting cranked. In business, the same argument applies. It is really necessary to have some time to consolidate your position and evaluate your progress. There is little to be gained by leaving behind a series of many half-evacuated moves, as opposed to a few which were fully successful.

3. **Be sure of where you are going.** If there is more than one principal in the business, make sure that all have a common goal and that their goal is to build a successful business. If one partner is playing hobby shop and another is looking for personal gratification, you can be sure that the business will go nowhere. At times it is fashionable in some

quarters to cast aspersions on strategic planning. That sort of thinking is nonsense. No one can count on good luck alone to carry the day. A better policy is to spend time thinking about what you want to do and what it takes to get it done, and then organizing your resources to get there.

4.   Protect your market position and exploit your customer base. It is far easier to keep a market share than build a new one. If you must build a new one, keep the old one alive as long as possible. It happens that people lose interest in their present business and spend their free resources in trying to get into new ones. Often the attempts are marginally successful and the old business looks a lot better than it did when the whole thing started, except that new people are now in the competition picture. The customer base is a gold mine of opportunity for selling spare parts, new equipment, and modifications of old equipment. It is also a gold mine of opportunity for public relations in the form of referrals from happy customers.

5.   Business is business. Don't give jobs to your friends simply because they are friends. Bring in the best people you can find and let your employees evaluate new people before you bring them in. There is nothing more devastating to an organization than being saddled with incompetent management. The employees will see it even if the next level of management doesn't. The "old boy" system is for the birds. Reward your people well and expect a lot in return. When you must correct an error in hiring or a deficiency in production, do it quickly and decisively face to face. One proviso: there is a place for most people, and while creating a job should only be done if there is an authenticated need, sometimes people who fail in one arena can be winners in another. Most employees on the verge of extinction deserve to be considered in this light. There are exceptions which do not need to be enumerated, and people who have failed in their obligations should be quickly excise from the group.

6.   At some point in a company's life, raising money usually becomes a necessary part of doing business. The trick, assuming you have a company and products sufficiently attractive to investors, is to raise money when you don't need it. There is nothing less attractive than a company which is broke and in a panic to attract investment, and you haven't lived life to the fullest until you have had to make a payroll with about six bucks in the bank. This is not an experience to be savored, and one's gastric condition and sanity can be protected if it is avoided completely. Cash-flow, fortunately, can be projected, assuming the management is actually in control of the process. The time to start planning the next big hit on the financial market is the day after the last financing. The time to do public issues is when the company is difficult to evaluate. Once a stable position is attained, the attractiveness of the company as an investment declines, and the good old price-earnings ratio comes into play. If I could pick my time for any offering, it would be a time of rapid expansion, new product introduction, and rapidly declining losses.

7. **Treat investors' money better than you would treat your own.** Spend it on the programs that were the basis for their investment and don't throw money after projects which would be better off dead. Everyone is sympathetic toward losses if the losses are incurred in pursuit of a goal and if progress is being made. Spending money to keep a losing business afloat while doing nothing about the source of the problem is gross mismanagement.

8. **Inventories are killers, and there is money to be made in good inventory management.** It is sometimes easier to let the sleeping dog lie, but it is also expensive. One reason inventories get out of hand is that people who develop products can rarely resist making improvements, sometimes on improvements which have just been released. This is controllable by good configuration management, and every successful company avoids flushing inventory down the tube each time a bright guy comes up with another modification. There is no moral requirement to get improvements into products unless the purpose is to correct an urgent sales situation or to provide a suitable margin of safety. If the present configuration can hold its own in the market and does not damage users, then there is good argument for getting an effective date for the new configuration which allows inventory to be used effectively. There are very few good arguments for introducing a new circuit board when a new version of one that works was just recently the subject of a multi-thousand-dollar purchase order.

9.   Most cases where stealing occurs in the purchasing department happens as a direct result of poor procedures, often coupled with excessively centralized administration. If the purchase order tracks the request, the purchase, the delivery, the invoice and the payment, and these steps are sufficiently decentralized in their approval and review, little opportunity for fraud is available. Kick-backs are probably best stopped by varying the purchasing procedure so that there is not a continuing relationship between buyer and vendor. In dealing with cases of this type, get competent legal help. There are traps in these situations, and even though proof is at hand, you may be constrained in what you can do and say.

10.   Audits are mandatory in business, and outside auditors are a must. Outside auditors bring a detached outlook to the process, and if they are good, will help a lot in formulating management policy relative to the fiscal affairs of the company. Auditors also help in keeping things honest, but that is a minor part of what they do for the company. They will concentrate on your procedures and recommend policies which will protect your assets and earnings. It is not really necessary to have one of the very large accounting firms as your auditor. Many small local firms are just so good. In the case of public companies, it is customary to get a big-name auditor, but I have always suspected that there is no real reason for this. People in the financial world are prone to overkill.

11.   Everyone has a computer system, and there are advocates for every type and for every software package. What is important is that the system and its software give you what you need to run the company. Computers do not make errors. People make errors. Software bugs make errors, but most of the catastrophic type show up early in the testing process. If you buy established packages, you probably won't encounter other than minor bugs. It is very important that a business be able to project its business for a while ahead. Projecting for the duration of the backlog is easy. Projecting a year ahead of the backlog is hard and requires information not available in the books. Projecting ahead for five years is probably a daydream but can be useful if one bases the projection on demographics, industry trends, planned product posture changes, acquisitions, and so on. Planning should be an annual affair. Failures of the projection process within a quarter demands immediate action to define the cause. Surprises are inherently bad. If you are smart, you will dislike surprises whether they are good or bad, since surprises occur in a void of information. One note of caution: in changing business software packages, bite the bullet and run the two packages in parallel for a while. Who needs a midnight call from the controller telling you that the quarter's records have gone up in smoke?

12.   A good board of directors can be very useful if anyone listens to them. The most pointless thing on earth is collecting a roomful of trophy or diversity directors and then managing the company as though they weren't there. A good board will immerse itself in the details of the company's performance and will call the management to account for poor results or bad practice. In some cases, a board will help provide direction to a company, but those cases are probably in the minority and should be so if management is doing its job. A board, more than anything, provides oversight. If the board is doing its job, this oversight will be detailed and demanding. In general, the shareholders of public companies are one of the worst-served groups extant. There is a tendency for boards to be selected by management for their compliance and for other reasons which inhibit their objectivity. Consequently, CEOs tend to be overpaid and under-stressed, and the shareholders pays the bills. Any CEO not producing a fair return on equity and a suitable profit on operations should not only be deprived of a bonus but should be fired. I can think of very few cases where this has actually happened in the absence of a change of control, but every year we read about many cases where a CEO is handsomely rewarded for minuscule accomplishment. Boards need a degree of independence similar to that we expect from auditors, but that may be too much to expect.

13.   Any organization should maintain a capital equipment inventory and depreciation schedule. It goes without saying that capital equipment disposal procedures should be documented and adhered to and that these actions should be coupled back into the accounting system. Such policies are in the responsibility of the CFO, and any organization, no matter how small, needs this function. When the company is embryonic, the function is usually served by one of the principals. If none of the principals are competent in this area, the accountant or controller can provide the basics and the lack of financial expertise at the top can be accommodated by means of consulting services usually available from accounting firm. When the critical mass is reached, a CFO is needed, and a good one will pay for himself. I have never seen a successful business which did not have good financial reporting. The chickens really come home to roost when a company is faced with the need for financing and cannot justify its results and asking price.

14. In hiring people, one should always keep open the option of over-hiring in skill level. When a company is in growth mode, it is a certainty that the time will come when the overqualified staff member becomes simply fully qualified for the next evolutionary stage. I have always maintained that you can evaluate a person fully by an appraisal of the people who surround that person. A bad manager will surround himself with people who are worse than himself, apparently on the basis that they will make him look good. The best executive I have ever seen are surrounded by people of overwhelming competence and intelligence. These executives know that the way to look good is to produce results, and the way to produce results is by the application of the best resources available.

15. The truth is your most powerful tool. It is not necessary to do a continuous memory dump, but it is necessary to be honest and straightforward with your people and with your investors. In a public company, there are rules about what you say and how you say it, but these rules generally do not inhibit your treating investors like you are glad they put their money into the enterprise. A company makes its reputation on results, but it is hard to imagine a company with a reputation for dissembling, poor customer service, and bad shareholder relations ever getting to the point where good results were an issue. One thing we take with us wherever we go is our reputation. It is like our shadow, and both are visible whenever we are held up to the light. When your word is good, the world is saved a lot of time since no one has to waste it trying to figure out what you are saying. I have seen a lot of big deals made on a handshake, with the implicit assumption that the details can be all worked out later. This is only possible when the right people are doing the shaking. The same argument applies to your employees. It isn't necessary to say too much, but when you say something, make it stick.

16. Research and development can be a corporate welfare program which has no function other than keeping a bunch of otherwise unemployable longhairs at work. The trick is to make research and development directly responsive to the purpose and market posture of the company. I am not impressed with the argument that many inventions succeed by accident. One of the examples often referred to is that of the semi-sticky labels marketed by 3M. It is too easy to forget that the glue was a failed version of a type being developed for another purpose, and that the product itself was conceived in a stroke of marketing genius. The research and development programs of a company need to be attached to something within the company and should be funded out of individual product line revenues. This keep the process honest. It helps if there is a review procedure which asks "why are we doing this?" and "where are we going?", but only if the budgeting process is clear enough that one can understand what is happening. Research and development cannot be evaluated by the number of patents filed or number of papers published. It isn't hard to get a paper published or get a patent issued from the Patent Office. The results that count are those that leak out of the lab into the market position of the company. All the rest is vanity, and one should not lose sight of the fact that tax deductibility returns less than a third of the cost. The rest comes out of the corporate pocket.

17. Business success in a new company is heavily affected by luck and opportunity. Neither of these stands alone, however, since turning either luck or opportunity into success requires aggressive action on the part of management. This is generally the reason why both of these factors diminish in importance as companies grow older and larger. When a business is relatively new, it is easy for creative people to get the ear of top management, and management generally understands the business. In a larger company, it often happens that the opportunity expires before the idea drifts up to the level where someone can make a decision. Fate does not distribute opportunity from a salt shaker but drops it at infrequent random intervals. When one of these apples of opportunity drops into the corporate lap, quick action is in order. All this is not to say that the environment for opportunity and luck cannot be affected by corporate action. The apocryphal story about Newton might be different if he had been somewhere other than under the apple tree, but he would probably have figured it all out anyway. In the case of a corporation, however, it is necessary to position the company so that good things might occur. A friend once said that his father told him not to marry for money, but to go where money was when looking for a wife. A corporation which keeps the right company in the right industry positions itself to capture opportunity and to experience luck.

18. Founders are a blessing and a curse. The computer business is littered with the remains of companies whose founders rode the same horse until it died. Business is dynamic, and the forces of an industry, contrary to what some founders think, are not confined within one's own corporate structure. The best money one can spend is on marketing. Sales are another matter, but if marketing does its job, selling will take care of itself, assuming the sales staff is kept hungry and on the road. Marketing consists largely of marketing analysis and definition of product posture. No one expects marketeers to invent anything, and if they are thinking at this level, they should be fired. On the other hand, if the industry is locked into bench-mounted frames testers, it should be the marketeers who discovers that the world is crying for a hand-held device. If the technical group discovers an anti-gravity machine, anyone can reason out that there may be a market for it. If the product is less profound, then marketing should be capable of discerning the interest and probable market, given some specifications and probable price. Even the latter is suspect coming from engineers. In recent years, the Japanese have done things backwards. It once was that engineers conceived the product and stated the price. Market research then explored the market. It was not long ago that you could buy a nice FAX machine for ten thousand dollars or so. Under the new thinking process, the market was redefined in terms of what would happen if the price were in hundreds rather than thousands of dollars, and the rest is history. We see this every day now in the proliferation of inexpensive products flooding the market. Unless a product is absolutely irresistible, price and market are tightly linked. If a product is truly irresistible, jack up the price and plan on a larger bank account. Don't take an engineer's word for the irresistibility, however.

19. Back to founders, for a moment. Just because you start a company doesn't mean you have all the answers. If you do your job, you will hire a lot of people smarter than you are, and common sense says you should listen to them now and then. It wouldn't hurt to read the papers, also. As the company grows, the founders should take a different role and become leaders rather than doers. If the founders have political, environmental or social causes as their motivation, they should confine these to their personal lives. If they cannot, then they should leave the company and let it grow and thereby provide them with the wherewithal to pursue these interests.

20. There is a saying in the stock market which advises letting your winners run and cutting short your losers. The same applies to business. If a product line simply isn't making it, kill it before it kills you. If a verifiable opportunity exists in another direction, heap on the resources and establish a market. There are very few cases where one can actually buy a market. If the company has unlimited funds, it can be done, but why bother? My contention is that any business worth pursuing must be profitable. Sometimes people convince themselves that there are other reasons for staying in a market, but I haven't seen many cases where this has really worked out. Generally, there are other ways to fill the wagon, such as OEM arrangements which bring in products from other companies. The beauty of this situation is that the other guy takes all the real risk. If you decide to pursue a new direction, then don't kill it by insufficient funding. There is a common tendency to underestimate the resources required to get a product to market, and nothing is more enervating to project dynamics than to suffer from financial starvation. In for a penny, in for a pound, as the old saying goes.

21. There is a fundamental law of business which should be engraved on the desk of every CEO. This law says that the business posture of a company should be under its own, and that no outside agency should be able to harm the company's business by its actions or inactions. This law is the basis for alternate sources of critical components, for example. If your primary product is an attachment to another company's product, be prepared for the day when that product disappears or incorporates a feature which makes your product unnecessary. If your product incorporates a sub-assembly for which there is no substitute, brace yourself for trouble. Few manufacturers feel constrained to issue early warnings about discontinuance of products or of large price increases. The best of all worlds is a product posture which is based on standalone products built of components available anywhere.

22. I should carry the preceding paragraph a step further. OEM arrangements are frequently of unequal value to buyer and seller. Any company buying OEM products which form a substantial part of their sales picture will sooner or later turn their thoughts to the question of how to rid themselves of the OEM partner. It is also a given that there is little benefit in sharing future plans with that partner except insofar as these plans intersect the status quo. If supplying OEM products to others is a major part of a company's business, the company is perpetually in danger of unexpected body blows, assuming that the OEM product has no life of its own. There is a similar argument regarding royalty income. A lawyer in the licensing business once told me that royalties are like something like a persistent itch. They won't kill you, but they are something that are worth getting rid of. Consequently, one can expect the licensee to devote some time to the notion that the licensor is expendable.

23. Getting information is the key. It is amazing how many people providing services to companies regards themselves as business wizards without, for the most part, ever getting their hands soiled in the real thing. There is some good advice available from these people, but their function generally ends at their specialty. Business is not complicated, by and large, and it doesn't take a genius to identify destructive behavior on the part of management. Getting information is the key and showing up for a quarterly board meeting does not pass muster in this regard.

24. Business intelligence is analogous to military intelligence, but with less bloodshed. It is imperative that a company knows what the market is doing, what the competition is doing, and what business partners are doing. Sale and marketing people should be trained in the function and it should be part of their job description. One of the things they should learn is there is probably more to be learned from customer service people and others at that level than from the VP of sales. The latter person won't tell you anything, whereas the chances are good that no one ever told the service personnel to not pass along rumors.

25. My partner and I always took the position that we would maintain a very close relationship with our financial supporters, but that board meetings were not a place where these people should be represented. One of the predominant characteristics of people in the financial word is there high opinion of themselves. Venture capitalists usually seek a seat on boards of companies in which they invest, probably with the motivation of protecting their investment, and investment bankers will do the same if given the opportunity. There are some exceptions, and I have met all kinds. Given the opportunity for embarrassment and conflict of interest, it is probably better on average to keep them away.

26. Lawyers are pretty valuable, but it is rare to find one with real business sense. A problem with the legal profession is an inability to close with the likelihood question. If every step in life is governed by the down side, then progress will be made in very small steps indeed. I don't advocate risk which can get one into the slammer, but I do advocate allowing the possibility that every potential outcome need not be covered in an agreement. When an agreement is to be made, the business terms should be laid out by the principals, and the lawyers should reduce it to writing. Unfortunately, many lawyers cannot resist the impulse to be creative, which often results in the corruption of the business terms. This is a tendency which needs to be nipped in the bud. When it is all said and done, any agreement is generally the basis for future disagreement, since the language itself is imperfect. All you can do is try, and the real protection lies in the integrity of the people making the agreement. When chiseling starts, walk away.

27. A measure of maturity is being able to do unpleasant jobs in a civilized and objective way. There are many so-called managers extant who are afraid to face difficult problems with employees and consequently let bad situations continue long after discovery. Terminating an employee is a difficult action, but it is made far more difficult by not facing the problem head-on. The interview should be brief, to the point, objective and business-like. Once the decision is made, the deed should be done, and the employee should be out of the plant the same day. The same argument applies to any other unpleasant job. These jobs never get easier or better through delay, and in fact are somewhat like over-age eggs in this regard.

28. Products make the wheels turn. There are many companies suffering from the "empty wagon" syndrome in that their product catalog is not extensive enough to enhance the salesman's chance of making a sale. In this regard, one should note that sales people will generally sell the products which are easy to sell, and it is worth contemplating different sales methods and commission structures when products are quite diverse. A company cannot survive without innovation, since competition will otherwise force its products into extinction. Corporate profits which are substantial but based on an expense structure which does not include adequate product development will not be maintained. A healthy product mix aimed at different markets segments with a continuum of new products and product improvements make a company a tough competitor.

29. Find the right bank and worm your way to the top. The last people you want to deal with are loan officers of the lesser type, so the best strategy is to capture yourself a Senior Vice-President. A friend in a very large accounting firm one told me that most finance graduates start out in banks, and those who can't do anything else stay there. That may be a bit harsh, but you can't beat bankers for parochial outlook. If you can't find a path to senior management in the bank you're dealing with, find another bank. The junior people have a big handbook of "cans" and "cant's" which they won't show you but which defines every action they take. What you want is someone who will share your vision and put a little weight on the skill and probity of your principals.

30. Don't put your corporate money into real estate until you have more money than you need. Personal money is another thing entirely. The problem with real estate as a corporate investment is that the rate of return is too low, under average conditions, compared to the other things one can do with the company checkbook.

31. Every business principal needs an exit strategy. It is no accident that most technical innovation is done by younger people, nor that people get tired of chasing the same set of problems after a long period of time. Exit strategy is made easier by being a public company, in view of the liquidity available if the company survives. Survival can be enhanced by the maintenance of a good succession plan, and this is important under any circumstances. If the principal exits the hard way, a good succession plan can assure that the survivors and family have a good shot at the future. If the process is less painful, good succession planning provides the same advantage. Acquisition is the preferred exit route for founders of smaller companies, and alternatives in this arena should be continuously evaluated. Merger needs to be done under the quickest and cleanest circumstances. Founders therefore should guard their majority ownership jealously and resist giving away excessive amounts of equity. The best of all worlds is to have majority ownership in the hands of very few people who have a common goal.

32. One of life's big mysteries is why companies divest themselves of perfectly good, profitable subsidiaries on the grounds that the business is too small to worry with. I have always felt that there is a very good solution: find a good manager, give him some goals for profitability, give him a big piece of the action, and tell him to send you an audited financial statement each year. If things continue to prosper, the parent will reap the benefits and the manager will get wealthy. The total investment in management's time, if they are smart enough to leave the subsidiary alone, is the time it takes to read the financial statement and deposit the money. I have always felt that there is a measurement of arrogance in those situations where the CEO is simply too busy to think about a small but profitable division. Money is money.

(Thank you, Jack.)

CONCLUSION

A wise man once told me that at the end of the day "(B)e thankful for what you have passed and be thankful for what you have before you."

We learn from our past, we live in our todays, and we hope for our tomorrows.

This book is just a primer; while it is not a magic lamp to grant you your wish of success, it can give you tools to use to chase your dreams - but you have to implement them and do the work yourself if you want to go from just reading about having your own business to actually running your own successful, profitable, start-up small business.

Most people make a "livelihood" – a term Merriam-Webster's defines as being your "means of support or subsistence." This is basically working for enough to pay your bills, but not more. To move beyond just paying your bills and to get to where you are living the America dream, you need more. Like from the walls of my old school, you need to always work toward your "Good Better Best," doing for "Others" and telling the truth, or at least being honest with yourself and your stakeholders; the people who rely on your business: owners, suppliers, employees and customers. Success is mostly hard work accompanied by some fortune and luck, and the foresight to be planned and prepared for each and every contingency, emergency, and blindside that comes your way. Prepare enough, be smart about your finances and your financing, get help when you need it, and put in the effort, and there is literally no ceiling to what you can accomplish. Look at entrepreneurs like Bill Gates, Elon Musk, Warren Buffett, Steve Jobs, Hewlett and Packard, and others who had little but became wealthy because they had an idea, a strong business plan, solid financial preparation, and helpful investors. And they did the work. Always remember that.

As Andrew always says, "There is always a way, if you can find it."

So work hard and find it. We found it. This Book is proof!

And when you do find it, let me know if I was of any help to your success. I'd love to be able to talk about your story in my next book. The one on how I failed retirement. (Four times and counting....)